Managing Annoying People

7/17

Dear ▓▓▓,

Thanks for attending my session at SLA! Amazing, not Annoying -- free Book since we ran out! Would love if you could write a review on Amazon!

Irene

MANAGING ANNOYING PEOPLE

7 PROVEN TACTICS TO MAXIMIZE TEAM PERFORMANCE

Ilene Marcus, MSW, MPA

ISBN-13: 9781530496266
ISBN-10: 1530496268
Library of Congress Control Number: 2016919630
CreateSpace Independent Publishing Platform
North Charleston, South Carolina

To my daughter, Samantha Elizabeth --
who always knows just what to order.
Love you first.

ACKNOWLEDGMENTS

No book is ever accomplished alone. I want to thank all of my friends, family, peers, colleagues, therapists, self-help groups, and random people who walked with me (OK, sometimes we drove; often we just sat on barstools) on my path to fulfilling my unique contribution. You know who you are and have my devotion. If that's not enough for you, please refer to the chapter on boundaries.

A few special shout-outs are unavoidable. To my Mom, whose unfaltering love may show up as annoying, from time to time. Henry DeVries, for teaching me how to build the path. Karen and Christie Glasbergen for the rights to use Randy's cartoons. Bob Harding for always having his eye on the target. And Chickie Piazza, the eternal believer.

Contents

FOREWORD

L eadership is one of my favorite topics. Having strong beliefs and being able to stick with them through popular and unpopular times is the most important characteristic of a great leader. These attributes bring out the best in us and others. They ground us, reminding us of our most important principles. They inform us about where we should be heading as a society. As a leader, I try to bring out the best in people around me and in turn they bring out the best in others, and we all do better as individuals and a society.

Throughout my career I have addressed many difficult situations. I had to count on my team and make sure I had the right people in the right place at the right time. During my tenure as Mayor, reforming New York City's welfare system was a major priority for me. When I entered office in 1994, a full 20 percent of all New Yorkers were on the welfare rolls. A shocking one out of every five New Yorkers was depending on government assistance! I was taught the value of hard work from my parents. I wanted to provide opportunities and end the cycle of dependency. The scope of the problem was huge. That's when I met Ilene Marcus, full of moxie and the tenacity to get the job done.

My goal was to revamp one of the largest bureaucracies in the nation. Ilene was a born manager, sophisticated enough to understand the policy, budget and mandates; savvy enough to line up all of the operational issues and carry out the work with staff that was already in place. There is no substitute for personal experience when dealing with problems. Leadership is about finding and making that experience your own. Ilene was able to take it a step further to make it a team experience. We had a steady decline in the rolls over the four years Ilene spearheaded the program, putting more New Yorkers back to work, improving the parks and other public spaces and providing opportunity where none had existed before.

"Managing Annoying People" puts a complex management issue into perspective. It's not just about good performance. It's the idea that great leaders know how to get the best out of their people regardless of the setting, the circumstances and the timing. Getting the most value out of your investment in your employees should be at the top of every leaders list. "Managing Annoying People" taps into real truths that Managers face every day and provides a roadmap to be your best self and guide your team to stay the course and get the job done.

Rudolph W. Giuliani

INTRODUCTION

---

*The task of the leader is to get his people from
where they are to where they have not been.*

HENRY A. KISSINGER

The core competency of management is to truly appreciate your staff and make the team more powerful than each individual.

Why write about managing annoying subordinates? Bad managers are like bad teachers; they leave an imprint, make each day miserable, and make it difficult to find the joy in the work. The ripples of their impact outlast the work relationship and often set the foundation for the next work relationship. Being valued and appreciated with a sense of fairness is a key human emotional driver, regardless of your generation and its concurrent values.

Gen Xers, millennials, and now pluralists bring focus to the murky issues of work and purpose. They crave purpose and will not compromise it for quality of life. Now, in their twilight years, baby boomers who spent most of their lives working to build economic security desire balance and fun. On this point, the generation gap does not exist. Finding inspiration, kindness, and purpose in the workplace is always relevant.

CEOs, C-suite executives, and managers have essential roles in setting the workplace atmosphere. The outright power differential and economic contract implicit in the boss-subordinate relationship makes it like no other. The lessons endure. They make an imprint. And we all want more.

Coaching leaders to build powerful cohesive teams is a step to building a better company and then a better world. The goal is for managers to create a work environment filled with joy and purpose and watch the phenomenon multiply.

This book will make you think about the managers you've had, the lessons you've adopted from them, and how they have shaped your work life. It will prompt you to dig deep about who you are as a manager and to picture yourself in circumstances that are eerily familiar. If I have done my job right, this book will spur managers to handle situations in new ways. To think about how words and actions make a lasting imprint.

Let's be crystal clear about the power dynamic in the boss-subordinate playing field. The power struggle is not about anything covered in an antidiscrimination clause. One player is the boss, and one is not. Whoever said in the sandbox, "You're not the boss of me," was wrong when it comes to workplace structure.

This book is organized by tactic, each with several ideas on how to change your boss-subordinate relationship patterns. Next in each chapter, a scenario embodies the tactic and supports the concept by bringing together ideas with actions. You may think these actions will differ depending on whether they relate to a for-profit business, non-profit, government, or start-up. You may think the sector and lines of business matter. They don't. Human behavior patterns between managers and employees matter. These vignettes showcase how you can introduce new relationship patterns.

Go forth, and be audacious.

CHAPTER 1

The Trap of Annoying Subordinates

Managing Annoying People, 2017. By **Ilene Marcus**

Annoying is subjective. We all experience annoying differently. Many books and articles discuss various types of annoying people and provide suggestions to address *their* behaviors. You know the type: the excessive talker, the know-it-all, the "maybe" guy, and—my favorite—the martyr. All of these books are on point about what is annoying, but none directly discusses the relationship if one of you is the boss and the other the subordinate. This drastically changes the dynamic, as the power differential should be in your favor. Annoying people who report to you do more damage than just annoying you. They steal your time and energy.

As a leader, you are not the only one stuck in the trap. When your productivity falters, so does the productivity of your team. Being a senior manager is about setting the direction and steering the entire ship to that destination. If you get sidetracked, the entire enterprise can fall off track. If your staff drains you, you cannot stay focused on achieving results. The plot thickens when you add in the team, and the time drain multiplies.

It's a common scenario. Someone who works for you pushes your buttons. You get annoyed at whatever he or she says or does. Whether it's a generational habit, a quirky trait, or just the way he says hello, you are irritated. It doesn't impact the person sitting next to you or anyone else in the room. Just you. You, the direct manager of this person. You are responsible for his performance, not his idiosyncrasies. You must manage his work. He is good at what he does, but his behavior irritates you. And it wastes time. The time waster is the trap, and the energy it drains is the monster problem.

In conversations with CEOs, C-suite executives, and senior managers, I have seen a disconnect between management level and the amount of time wasted on managing annoying subordinates. Why is it more of a concern to C-suite execs and senior management and less of a hot topic for CEOs? The reason is that most CEOs have options. CEOs can put distance between them and the annoyer. The C-Suite exec or other senior manager may not be able to pawn the worker off onto another level of management, especially if the person was already reassigned by the CEO. The reality is, if the employee is providing value (bringing in customers and bucks), it will be a game of musical chairs, and eventually someone will be stuck managing the annoying employee.

Overwhelmingly, managers respond in the same manner upon hearing the topic *managing annoying people*: immediate knowing smiles, nodding heads, and then hearty laughs. Tag, you're it.

Managing annoying people is truly relevant in today's workplace. In an environment where employees are competent, moral, and ethical and bring real value, managers are challenged to cope with numerous social skill sets and employee styles and eccentricities that can annoy to no end.

Now, get ready. Throughout the book, examples are used to illustrate points and tactics. Many of these are from my personal, firsthand experiences as a C-suite exec and coach. Some are poignant stories from colleagues and others who have sought my assistance. Several are composite situations based on real stories and personalities.

Management Styles Are Public

With the advent of websites capturing employee reviews and sentiments about the companies they work in, combined with networking platforms and social media tweeting away, hiring and firing trends are public. Pluralists, millennials, and Gen Xers are not shy about advertising their experiences. Managers cannot afford to be cavalier about how they treat their workers or about terminating those who annoy them.

Ilene, Chief Operations Officer
The lifeblood of all companies is the staff. As COO for a health care company in NYC, Ilene (yes, that's me) was responsible for

ensuring full staffing for physical therapists to meet mandated service levels. The company set competitive compensation and was recruiting on all cylinders, including two internal dedicated staff members trolling the job boards, contracts with staffing agencies, and an employee-referral program. Nothing doing. As COO I needed to do something quickly. We were losing revenue and were out of compliance. I checked Glassdoor, and there it was: "hostile work environment." It was true. On a day-to-day basis, the therapists would never even interact with the CEO, but when they did, and the CEO didn't agree with their candid feedback, he became hostile and a screamer. There was no applicant pool.

Candidates today do their homework first and listen to their peers' and colleagues' experiences.

Flying Solo without Human Resources

Even with formal processes such as the annual 360-degree performance review and the resources devoted to employee development and training, on a day-to-day basis, relationships are tested. Incompetence, insubordination, and outright outlandish behaviors are grounds for dismissal, and Human Resources (HR) will be right by your side. However, if you can't put your finger on why a person annoys you, or if it's a personality clash, HR may not be a resource. It doesn't matter if you work in a small enterprise or a large organization; the expertise, time, and timing may just not be available from HR.

Managers are confronted with countless situations that aren't necessarily the purview of the HR team. Someone who gets the job done and is moral and ethical but pushes your buttons and impacts your team dynamic is more complicated to deal with. In this fast-paced work world of remote meetings and focus on outcomes, as long as results are being achieved, the CEO and HR may tend to let it go. More than ever managers have to face situations that don't follow conventional rules. Even when a high level of emphasis is placed on developing a positive workplace culture, there is always a bump in the road and a work relationship that will need to be addressed. That's when the manager is most likely flying solo.

Charlie, Chief Development Officer
In a major philanthropy, Barbara joined the team as director of major gifts from a competitor and clearly was a star. Her fund-raising techniques were legendary. In her first month, she brought on two new major donors, each committing $1 million.

In this business, even the stars crunch their own data. Barbara refused to do this. Given her reputation all eyes were on her, and the CEO really didn't understand the full extent of the process necessary for tracking fund-raising activities. Charlie, the chief development officer, was Barbara's direct manager and reported to the CEO. He was in a bind with a high performer who was bucking the work culture.

Over Barbara's first two months, Charlie met with her about the reporting process several times. Barbara always promised Charlie she would update the database and that she understood the importance of the reports. Every week there were excuses about why the numbers were not completed. Six months later there was no data, and Charlie was really annoyed. He needed a plan to harness Barbara's talent while making sure her style fit into the company's culture and the data was tracked. It was clear to Charlie that all were watching with his new star player, and he was on his own to figure this one out.

Generations Collide

Let's start with the basics. Boomers are the oldest; next are Gen Xers, followed by millennials and then the newest generation to hit the workplace: pluralists. Each group's core values and experiences impact its members' work styles. Millennials and pluralists have never known a work world without smartphones and social networks. They are often opinionated without having a lot of backup data, as they have been the focus of marketing efforts since years before they actually had their own money to spend. Because of their exposure to media and attachment to electronics, they are used to driving priorities and setting their own agendas. Millennials are documented as the most ethnically diverse generation and are more accepting of differences. They tend to be self-assured, as they were raised by helicopter parents who instilled in them that they are special and should reach for their dreams. And if they don't reach their dreams, there are large safety nets and trophy collections just for showing up.

This has a huge significance in the workplace, where those baby-boomer bosses born between 1946 and 1964 believe success is a straight path tied to effort. Gen Xers, millennials, and pluralists, hatched between 1965 and 1997, view the world from the perspective that optimism isn't always tied to effort. They know how to look at their roles and contributions concentrating on their values and have very distinct boundaries in the workplace, especially in relationships. The generational divide has never been more relevant.

Colleen, Executive Assistant
Every pair of eyes in the room turned to face me. With over one thousand people in seats, it was the first all-manager meeting this infamous NYC bureaucracy held. As I walked

from the stage wing to the podium, I had only one thought. Why hasn't my assistant showed up yet? A true millennial, Colleen was always attached to her phone. Even more annoying, there was no response when I called her. She knew this meeting was critical, and the tone it set would make or break the mayor's priorities I was responsible for implementing.

As my assistant, Colleen had worked painstakingly with me on this presentation. I wanted to share this moment and thank her publicly. She wasn't there. I was annoyed. Later that afternoon, with the congratulatory e-mails flying around, she came into my office grinning from ear to ear, extremely pleased with the outcome. I snapped, "Where were you?"

The young millennial said, "I knew you were prepared, and you had this. Everything was set. The walk-through was flawless. There was nothing else I could do. I chose to sleep in since you didn't need me."

Niche Specialties

You can't live with them, and you can't live without them. Workers who have niche specialties that you desperately need in order to achieve results are a rare commodity. The effect is even greater with youngins (millennials and pluralists) who feel bound to their own greater good and do not like to put up with situations that don't meet their standards.

Niche workers usually have extremely specific expertise, training, credentials, or experience that make them valuable. On the other hand, they may not display the array of attributes that make them invaluable, including being good team players, problem solvers, and decision makers. As their leader you must navigate this relationship to grow profits and workplace success while minimizing annoyance.

A lesson from the Reagan White House (what's a management book without a little presidential anecdote?):

There are many commentaries about the Reagan administration and Reagan's relationship to his cabinet. By all accounts Reagan had a competent team, each member with a special know-how. However, the inside scoop was that he did not like everyone in his cabinet. Many were East Coast elites, and Reagan was a ride-horses-and-chop-wood kind of guy. It would annoy him that some didn't enjoy a day at the ranch.

A hallmark of Reagan's leadership was to focus on the goals and make the relationships work regardless of personalities. His legacy—winning his second term with a record 525 electoral votes in a forty-nine-state landslide and approval ratings of 68 percent when leaving office, neck and neck with those of Franklin D. Roosevelt and later Bill Clinton—speaks for itself.

Results Rule

There is an old saying: data talks, BS walks. This has never been truer. There is no abatement of this phenomenon in sight. Future trends point to all data, including immediate consumer and end user information, being readily available with virtually no lag time.

Managers at all levels use data to make decisions. Data measures our teams' outcomes. Organizations need and value employees with outcomes who are contributing significantly to the core mission (and bottom line). Why are these employees always so annoying?

Stefanie, Volunteer Director
Over a three-year period, Stefanie, a top-performing millennial (twenty-two years old when she started) had grown the Volunteer Department in an iconic NGO human-services agency into a

benchmarked department that served as the hub for thousands of volunteers annually across New York City. I was her direct manager, and she kept me engaged in her activities.

Stefanie was demanding and asked for what she needed. "Can I have these resources? Can I miss the management meeting to attend a presentation? Why can't I sign my own purchase orders?" She followed the rules and exceeded outcomes. The program she built had an overwhelming return on investment (ROI) with funders, city administrators, and donors. It was revenue producing, and the press liked it and reported on it regularly. Yet every day, sometimes three or four times a day, I had to field questions from Stefanie and deal with them because I couldn't argue with the results.

The Connected One

They're the Voldemorts, if you will, of the corporate world. The words you still whisper. They're too scary to say outright. "I have the *connected one* working for me."

No situation is shocking in today's workplace. From nephews to ex-wives and lovers, from generous campaign donors' offspring to fellow churchgoers who are down and out on their luck, there is always someone who connects back to the Biggest Boss. Not a terrible fit for the job, but a square peg in round hole vis-à-vis your professional style. Quick refresher: annoying is not incompetent. Annoying is irritating behaviors in day-to-day situations that suck your energy. And this person is annoying, and you are stuck with her.

Ilene, Chief of Staff
At the very moment I needed to sit quietly and collect my thoughts, Andrea, a division chief and daughter of one of

our board members, approached me. If it were any other employee, after a ten-second scan of hot issues, I could prioritize the situation and decide to hold the conversation or not. With Andrea it was a little more complicated. I just didn't need the headache of worrying that she may say something to her father or play tennis with the entire executive committee that weekend and in passing mention how grumpy I was or that I seemed distracted. I engaged in the conversation and was immediately annoyed. This came across loud and clear. Now I was even more annoyed that I had the problem anyway.

Big town, small town—everyone is connected.

Ripples

As my dear friend Gary says to his wife, "Just because you are annoyed doesn't mean I am annoying." So true. It might not be the employee at all. It may be you. Just you. The way you experience this person and hear what he says, how he reminds you of someone else who gets under your skin. The truth is it just doesn't matter. What matters is how you react and how it impacts your time and productivity. A lot of people count on you at your workplace. If you don't have a plan to address these situations, it will be noticed. More importantly, those around you will feel the impact, and then everyone's time is wasted.

If you don't think you need to look at your own behavior toward certain employees, then don't read this book. On the other hand, have you ever left a management meeting or a conversation with a subordinate and wondered, why did I say that? What was that about? Why do I always take the bait and get into it with that person? Then you need help in managing annoying subordinates. Once you identify your annoyance level, the way you view your team and your management style will change forever. Are you ready for change? Perhaps. Is your team ready for you to change? Absolutely. Besides, you always need to keep them on their toes.

Checklist: The Trap of Annoying Subordinates

- Management styles are public and accessible by potential and current employees.
- Human Resources cannot always assist.
- Recognize the millennial and pluralist styles' impact on baby boomer and Gen X managers.
- Workers with niche specialties need special attention.
- Results come with more work and attention.
- Identify the connected one, and decide your plan of attack.
- Check the impact of your own actions.

CHAPTER 2

How to Prevent Annoying People from Sabotaging the Team

©Randy Glasbergen
glasbergen.com

T.E.A.M.

TOGETHER
EVERYONE
ANNOYS
ME

GLASBERGEN

Managing Annoying People, 2017. By **Ilene Marcus**

There are no generic solutions to specific problems. Each situation will need to be tackled one by one. The road to take is not to address what annoys you, but instead to follow the path of your reaction to the annoyance. How you handle behaviors that unsettle you is a lifelong challenge. How you handle annoying employees and keep their behavior from sabotaging the team is the test of a great leader.

In general, and all else being equal (no mental illness, life crisis, or other intangibles), people who are annoyed respond with one of four basic reactions, the Four Fs:

- Fight—you hit right back at the annoying employee, flinging the dirt, showing who's boss, and being difficult yourself.
- Flight—you turn and run, avoid at all costs, don't engage.
- Freeze—you feel stuck, not sure what to do or what to say, so you will ignore the annoyance.
- Focus—you gather your basket of tactics and manage full speed ahead.

Often, reactions to annoying subordinates are complicated and can overlap each other. How your team sees you react is more important than the annoying behavior that is disrupting the team.

Your goal is to focus. Use your prowess, and combine it with expertise to get out of the trap. You must set the tone as the team leader and minimize the office drama and impact on productivity. To do this you need to have annoying subordinates marching in tune with the rest of the band. And you need to be leading the team to a harmonious existence.

It takes a strong focus to wrestle this beast and not get caught in the trap. Too often we believe these situations will work themselves out. We reason that we are all competent, mission driven, and professional. With these three pillars in common, how can the situation get off track? The reality is, it can not only get off track, but it can become a full-blown train wreck. Understanding the impact to the team is essential to getting control over the beast.

The Forest and the Trees

Look at this through the forest lens. Individual trees make up the forest, but the forest is much more than each tree. It's an ecosystem wherein changes in one species impact the entire woodland. This is not just about your relationship with one direct report. The relationship is magnified by how the team sees you react to this person. It's fed with how they see you treat this person. It sets the stage for how they interpret your actions and then in turn decide how they should treat this person, each other, and, ultimately, you as the leader. Your action must be subtle enough to turn the situation in a new direction yet strong enough to make an impact on the entire team.

Model how you would like annoying team members to be treated. In meetings where the whole team is present, patterns are set and seen by all. You cannot assume that your team is behind you based on the facts. Your behavior is a variable you must take into account.

Brian, Chief Executive Officer
At the last three team meetings, Brian, the CEO of his family's flooring business, made snide comments to Mark, the sales director whose management style irritated Brian. The rest of the senior team agreed that Mark was annoying, but as the team witnessed the CEO berating Mark, they become sympathetic to Mark and viewed the CEO as the problem. There was a huge senior management turnover. The CEO didn't see the interrelationship between how he treated one staff member and how the rest of his

team processed his behavior. So he had very limited trees in his forest. Indeed, you could barely call it a forest.

Productivity Link

The key to understanding the impact on productivity is quantifying the amount of hours spent processing why you are annoyed, strategizing how to get less annoyed, and then recovering from being annoyed. To harness newfound time, energy, and rapport with your staff, you must fully appreciate what the annoying trap is currently costing you and the company. The payoff to overcoming the wasted time is renewed creativity, insight, and clarity of purpose. When you link your energy drain to the beast and to the rest of the team, you will be driven to master the skills of managing annoying behaviors that impede productivity.

Adam, Project Director
Adam's signature style was to be up against a deadline and then create turmoil throughout the office to complete the project. In their housing-development corporation, the work was intense and fast paced. Once the project was finished, it was all good. Quality aside, the chaotic process of watching Adam rush and engage three key personnel outside his department was downright irritating. Adam's manager had to constantly run interference across the departments due to the wake he was creating.

Post deadline, the manager would debrief with all involved, set a process for next time, and run more interference to get priorities that had been usurped back on track. Overall the annoyance took about four hours of management time every three weeks, including the wind-up and wind-down of the problem and the team debrief. Three senior managers spent an extra three hours on each episode that diverted attention from their core projects.

Quantify the time:

+	Manager time	= 4 hours	
+	3 sr. managers at 3 hours each	= 9 hours	
	Hours wasted	= 13 hours	
×	17 episodes over 52 weeks	= 221 hours wasted annually	

To add insult you can calculate the cost of the wasted hours:

+	4 hours manager time (calculated full in with benefits)	= $X
+	9 hours sr. managers' time (calculated full in with benefits)	= $Y
	Cost of hours every 3 weeks	= $X + $Y
×	17 episodes over 52 weeks	= 17 × ($X + $Y)
		$ wasted annually

Culture Bend

Your company's culture is embodied in the core mission, values, beliefs, and style of the founder and the management team. The culture is the intangible glue that holds all of the pieces of the company together in a cohesive package. It's the special sauce that makes the sum greater than all of the individual parts. It's executed through your policies, practices, and interactions between employees, customers, and business partners. Your employees feel it through compensation decisions, talent sourcing, investment in professional development, and emphasis on quality and ethics.

Culture fit is everyone's issue and yet no one's responsibility. The idea that like-minded individuals can work together more cohesively and enjoy work better is the gist of culture fit. In the most rudimentary understanding in the workplace, culture fit has been translated into a quick litmus test: Do I like this person? Do I want to spend time with them? It all comes down to how you define culture fit and what is truly valued in your workplace. For team cohesion, core values must be in alignment, such as passion about the work, a driving focus on success, ownership for one's actions, and a can-do attitude. It's inevitable that the culture will bend for those who are showcasing the company's core values when they do not submit to group norms.

Business development is a breeding ground for value-driven workers who create their own rules. Growing revenue in a for-profit, nonprofit, or association is key to keeping the company alive. Without new customers and services in business, new grants and donors in nonprofits, and new members in unions and associations, there will be no culture to nurture. And there's the rub. Sometimes the culture is adjusted for someone who is a rainmaker. The problem is he or she is usually raining on your parade and ruining your workflow. The culture bends for him because he is a necessary part of the revenue equation. And because you are a good manager, you make it work and hope no one else feels the pain.

Jenna, Customer Service Manager

Jenna was one of the strongest team members in a recreational facility where millennials ruled the roost. Her job was to be on the front lines from 9:00 a.m. to 5:00 p.m. True to her millennial style, her phone was always in her hand. Yet she set a boundary and didn't respond to noncrisis emails during the day. Dedicated and loyal, she burned the midnight oil getting back to her manager on a variety of issues that came up through the day. The manager was annoyed that a ranking team member couldn't get in the loop during the day. Jenna was clear that her priorities were the customers and on-site team management during the day. Her manager was more than cognizant that Jenna's daily activities fed the bottom line. Since Jenna performed excellently, the manager bent the rules and kept her on the leadership team. The manager and the other members had to work around Jenna's late-night e-mails.

Why Listen to Me?

I am annoying. It's true. I talk too fast, think too fast, and get to the heart of the matter quickly, probably before you want to get there. That makes me irritating. I also know that when your business is off track and you have tried a variety of fixes, when you are desperate and reaching the end of your rope, I am the one you call.

My management career went from zero to sixty miles per hour in the blink of an eye. Starting as a social worker advocating for change, then chosen as a top policy advisor to Mayor Rudy Giuliani when he took office in 1994, I was managing two interns until the mayor made me an offer I couldn't refuse. Welfare reform was one of Rudy's top three priorities in his first term. The mayor needed me to implement the policies and programs we had been planning. I was suddenly dropped into the deep end of the pool to manage a notorious bureaucracy with ten thousand staff and 1.1 million clients. A welfare system spiraling out of control. The mayor's management skills were legendary, and with his guidance, we were able to decrease the welfare rolls by seven hundred thousand during his first three years in office. Yes, the really deep end of the pool. Given my ramp-up time, I learned on the job.

My first and most important management lesson is this: Give people the tools and resources they need to do the job, and remove all the barriers in their way. Make sure employees have a clear path to accomplish their work. In 1994 the caseworkers (eight thousand of them) were making calls with rotary phones although touch-tone was already standard. How could they ever be productive? They could not dial more than ten calls an hour. With over 265,000 households to contact every six months, it was impossible to meet the goal. The long-term agenda was to provide job support for welfare participants to stay off of welfare and become independent. Short term, I had to get the workers making calls. Without the calls, the participants wouldn't know the steps they were expected to take to get to work. Besides, the union had a valid point: rotary phones were inefficient. As managers it's imperative to remove the barriers so the work can get done.

The second lesson is to make data and metrics your best friends. Math never came easily for me. I've always been highly analytical and inquisitive, but math challenges me. My career goals were to help people in difficult situations find community and assistance. I attained a BA in psychology and community change and then completed two master's degrees, one in social work and the other in public administration. I didn't want to help someone get a job; I wanted to change the whole system so everyone could get jobs. I needed to understand what drove decisions.

My first job was at the NYC Office of Management and Budget, overseeing the multibillion-dollar long-term care programs in NYC. Numbers were, ironically, now my life. However, once the suffering through financial modeling, spreadsheets, and macros was over, I realized that anything could be quantified. This is an amazing skill set that puts a manager in the driver's seat. Knowing your budget; the assumptions; and how to reconcile income, revenue, actions, and outcomes are critical management abilities. This is the second really important management lesson: know your numbers backward, forward, and in between, and quantify your team's efforts.

The third lesson came early on once I entered the management ranks. I wanted to be the type of manager people sought out for advice—the one who got the toughest jobs and the one who could solve a problem that had plagued generations before me. I wanted everyone to like me and want to work for me. What I found was that my employees liking me did not produce results. And that's the premise of my basic understanding of management. As a boss, I have an economic contract with each employee. As manager, my job is to provide the tools, resources, direction, and rules to help them meet their work obligations. Being inspirational, motivational, and wise are righteous perks once the minimum requirements are met.

All good management relationships are built on a foundation of clear role definition, expectations, and results. That's the basis of the work relationship between a boss and a subordinate, including a CEO and his direct reports. Nowadays there is much attention paid to leadership competencies, the skills needed to preform and motivate others. It doesn't matter if you graduated from business school or you had to learn on the job; you cannot divorce your management style from the basics. And the basics are: 1) identify the exact work expected of your employees; 2) clarify with employees for consistent understanding of roles and outcomes with management; and 3) ensure employees have the tools to meet these explicit expectations. Finally, review the results of what was accomplished based on the expectations, and make adjustments as needed.

Management styles may differ and workplaces evolve, but human nature remains constant. It is inevitable that someone on your team will annoy you. Be prepared. It's a good motto.

Checklist: How to Prevent Annoying People from Sabotaging the Team

- Connect the dots of your energy drain.
- Understand the four Fs and your responses.
- Understand the interplay between the individual and the team.
- Quantify the impact on the bottom line.
- Know when to bend the culture and when it's breaking.
- Listen to me. I know what I am doing.

CHAPTER 3

SEVEN PROVEN TACTICS

"As soon as we solve one problem, another one appears.
So let's keep this problem going for as long as we can!"

Managing Annoying People, 2017. By **Ilene Marcus**

The picture of how you relate to your staff is becoming clearer. You notice your reactions at a team meeting or when you address particular employees. You are starting to understand it. It's simple.

They annoy you. Fighting, fleeing, and freezing in your tracks haven't worked, or you would not have picked up this book. (By the way, thanks for reading.) Avoidance, complaints, and closer management have not changed the results. You are annoyed, and it's wasting your precious time. You need a plan that will transform the situation and put your universe back in order—and, of course, declare you as the leader of the pack.

These Seven Proven Tactics compose a toolbox of actions to sort the mess out with limited backlash and disruption of the work at hand. These tactics will maneuver you through an action plan to save time and money. Trust them, and they will guard your reputation and your sanity. These tactics will provide you with a blueprint to help you focus your reactions and plan your actions when dealing with annoying employees. They will guide you to staying productive.

These tactics can be used one at a time, in a grouping, or—my personal favorite—incrementally. Start slowly, and see if you can get the relationship on track. Escalate effort with additional tactics until you achieve the desired result. If you are not sure if it is working, have fun with it, and stage a test. Yes, you can set the trap instead of being trapped. Escalate accordingly.

Warning: These are powerful tools, and once you put them into motion you must see them through to completion. Aborting is not an option; it will exacerbate the situation and diminish your authority.

Tactic #1: Prevent Energy Suck

©Randy Glasbergen
glasbergen.com

GLASBERGEN

"I'm sorry, I wasn't listening. Can you repeat everything you've said to me since you started working here?"

Managing Annoying People, 2017. By **Ilene Marcus**

It's visceral. Your energy, spirit, and motivation are nonexistent after you meet with certain people. It's hard to put your finger on why. These are people you actually like, but when it comes to the work, there's always something, and meeting with them is draining.

You are the power player, and they know it. But they suck you dry. There is always a backstory or an explanation. A dynamic plays out that you have been denying. After your interactions with them or your avoidance of them, you feel you didn't own the situation or model executive behavior. That's the part that also sucks the rest of the day—wondering, why did I act that way?

The situation usually starts off innocently. For example, the scope of the project changes, and despite sitting three hundred feet from you, your director of field operations forgets to tell you about it. Or your top customer calls, and your head of contracts deviates on pricing because the customer says they have already spoken to you, and your subordinate doesn't want to waste your time. The mistakes are not big, but they put bumps in the road that you just don't need and would handle differently. They set a tone that doesn't set the pace for success. These subordinates are trusted and competent yet draining—oh, so very draining. And you can't stop it.

Don't Avoid

Books and experts will tell you what to do with people functioning with this modus operandi: avoid, avoid, avoid. This advice is really talking about family members, overzealous baristas, and peers. Unfortunately, this is not your scenario. You have an economic contract with this person. You provide financial compensation for him to perform a job according to your specifications. You cannot avoid him because he is too draining to manage. And no, you cannot avoid him, even if he gets 80 percent of it right and brings in millions of dollars each year.

Fran, Assistant Principal
Fran walks out of her office in an urban elementary school and spots Larry, the head custodian, walking toward her. She ducks back into her office. Fran likes and respects Larry. She is the Assistant Principal and shouldn't be ducking anywhere. But that's the impact Larry has on Fran. She knows he is going to complain about a tricky situation or ask a question that has more of a bite than she would like to answer. So Fran ducks.

Larry comes looking for Fran later in the day and actually asks, "Are you avoiding me?" Now, Fran is clearly not modeling executive behavior and is embarrassed. She has created two situations. First, a simple non-avoidance strategy—for example, saying, "Hi, Larry," keeping her head up, and walking on would have circumvented the "Why are you avoiding me?" conversation. And, more importantly, there's that feeling of not owning up to her role as Larry's manager and to how she should act. Thinking about the feeling sucks Fran's time.

Be Present

We all know the devil is in the details. If you check out during conversations with employees who annoy you, you will miss critical information, and important decisions will go amiss. It doesn't matter why they annoy you; it could be the way they present information, the amount of data they fling at you, or their overzealousness in attacking an issue. To tackle this you must be present, and that means getting specific.

This way of managing is annoying in and of itself. Even more so when it's a C-suite employee. When you tend to check out, the way to check back in is to be very specific and set the tone for the work. If you address the situation with generalities, the outcomes will wander away from you. Stand firm, and be specific. Ask detailed questions. Make sure you understand all of the moving parts. For example, you could ask, "What happens if the timing doesn't work?" or "Who will manage this part of the process?" If you find you have to ask plenty of questions to get the information you need, the answer may be a question more of competency than of annoyance. Make sure you can differentiate between the two. If it's competence, speak to HR. If it's your annoyance, get present and be specific. Asking questions in detail and getting specific will make you present.

Alan, Chief Financial Officer

Rebecca, director of member services at a union, was in charge of negotiating a multimillion-dollar multiyear contract. This was a complicated service program involving several locations and hundreds of staff serving thousands of union members. Rebecca had spreadsheets, analyses, and examples of new language and clauses for the contact. She wanted to start negotiating months early.

Every time she brought it to the attention of Alan, the CFO, his eyes glazed over because there was so much information. Rebecca was in the weeds, and Alan found her style of analyzing every aspect irritating. Instead of paying attention, Alan gave her his basic CFO language. As long as they covered the cost of all twenty locations and could meet deliverables, she could use her judgment.

Shame on Alan. What he should have done was ask specific questions about how Rebecca planned to cover the cost of all twenty locations and the allocated share of GM (general management). By checking out and not being specific, he did not leave room to figure out that GM was not in her equation. Rebecca was competent, so the contract on the whole was favorable. However, it opened up a huge cash hole for headquarters operations that Alan had to address.

Check In: If Quiet, Get Nervous—Very Nervous

It's natural to want to evade and circumvent situations that exasperate and irritate. So when all is quiet on the western front, you let sleeping dogs lie. Big mistake. Huge mistake. We all know that situations can rapidly grow and get out of hand. As managers our ability to differentiate between an issue that needs to be nipped in the bud and one that isn't quite ready to be pulled from the vine is critical. Indicators may vary among industries, but timing is always critical.

One indicator of that timing, especially with annoying subordinates, is quiet. I always know that something is about to erupt, based on my team members' personalities, if one of the players is quieter than usual. And you know which ones I mean: the annoying ones who get you every time.

Debbie, East Coast Chief

All week Debbie, the east coast chief, hadn't heard from Elyssa, the staffing director at an iconic jean retailer. Unusual behavior for Elyssa. Debbie easily got irritated with Elyssa and her needy behavior. However, she had so many hot situations on her plate; Debbie figured she would let it go another day. And another day. A week later, the director of HR came to ask why she had been circumvented when the hiring practice had been changed so that she no longer had to sign off on offer letters. The senior team was streamlining onboarding to get new hires on faster for the holiday season. At the last working group, Elyssa had deleted the step with a check and balance for HR to approve offer letters. If Debbie had checked in with Elyssa, she would have saved all the time that now had to be spent to right the process gone awry. Debbie's radar had gone up when Elyssa had gone radio silent, but she had ignored it to avoid irritation. Not good leadership on her part.

Use Documents

It's counterintuitive, because if you receive documents and material prior to the meeting, it will just make you more annoyed. It probably won't be as organized as you discussed or expected. Key information will be verbose, and it may not reconcile with the last report you reviewed—all part of the annoyance, because this employee does know what she is doing and produces results. By using documents at the meeting, although the content may not provide what you want, the conversation can drive the discussion instead of making you insane. Material at the meeting can be modified. You can use the conversation to shape the way it should look, get real-time data, and make notes (yes, you must make notes) on what you expect.

Tracking activities from meeting to meeting will build a better mousetrap.

Sarah, Director of Legislative Affairs
Sarah is a crackerjack. She is a born lobbyist. Her projects are always time sensitive, and she always comes through with flying colors. But the process is excruciating. Here's the analogy: She bakes a perfect cake, but she has to go back to the store so many times for so many different reasons. First, her shopping list is incomplete. Next, she goes to the wrong store. Then Sarah arrives five minutes prior to closing and doesn't have time to get everything she needs, and the list goes on. You can never tell from the finished project all the extra trips and work that she had to do because of her lack of planning; the cake is delicious. And I (her manager) always forget what it took to get there, and I eat the cake. When I use documents at the meetings with her, we can strategize and get rid of many of her detours, making the work process smoother and less painful.

Small Doses
Who says how long a meeting has to be? Santa Monica, California, is a leader in managing municipal parking. Years ago, prior to their

current metered-sensor system, individual meters were set oddly, at approximately eighteen-minute intervals. Why eighteen? Because a study was performed, and results showed that in downtown Santa Monica, eighteen minutes was the average time it took to run errands, including parking. The town could have rounded up or down for the metered time but chose to stick with the data they had found on optimal operations.

Figure out your optimal meeting time with your employees—an amount of time that balances getting the information or updates you need with ending the meeting when you are in a good zone and haven't reached your breaking point. Optimal team-meeting times for me are twenty- or forty-five-minute slots. Both of these times work much more efficiently than thirty- and sixty-minute slots. It communicates to the staff I am meeting with that I am under a time constraint, does away with the usual issue windup (which is usually when I start spiraling into annoyance mode), and accomplishes the end goal.

Adena, Project Assistant
A former genius millennial assistant of mine, Adena, calendared everything. She even put in "bio breaks." Adena was the one who analyzed my meeting behaviors and moved me to twenty- and forty-five-minute meetings. This left ten and fifteen minutes, respectively, every hour for bio breaks, phone calls, or emergencies. It also shortened my one-to-one direct-report meetings to less than two hours a week. Joy. Pure Joy.

Peer Meeting Format

Very few employees work in vacuums. As a matter of fact, a hallmark of successful leaders is getting staff out of their silos, so they understand the impacts of their actions on other divisions of the company.

When we get stuck in our interactions with annoying employees, we need to find ways to thaw the ice and take action. Peer meetings are an effective format to address the "work flow that gets stuck with this person because he annoys me" syndrome. This approach is different from grouping direct reports into project-based meetings where the work is clearly intertwined. In this format, schedule two people whose work informs the other with different management styles in the same meeting. When you are not alone in the room with a subordinate who annoys you and there is a peer of the annoying person also raising questions, it changes the dynamic. When a peer in a consultative manner queries, "Why did you do it that way? Did you consider XYZ? How about more information?" the questions are heard in a different way and usually acted on more succinctly.

Robyn, Benefits Director
Robyn directs a benefits program at a health-care company. Small changes in policy impact over three thousand people, most working remotely. Robyn is often so focused on the paperwork and compliance issues that she doesn't provide enough lead time to keep employees abreast of changes. We have discussed and planned several ways to inform employees, but her behavior is not changing, even after withholding bonus payment. I (her manager) instituted a peer meeting with Robyn and Lori, the director of regional operations. Lori innocently asked, "Why don't you alert managers first when there is a policy change, so we can manage our people?"

Robyn's eyes opened, as if she were hearing this for the first time. She responded, "I can alert managers or ask them for advice before completing changes and then not have to deal with all the fallout?" With only small lapses, this has not been an issue since.

Meeting with two subordinates at a time produces results.

Checklist: Prevent Energy Suck

- Don't avoid.
- Be present, and ask specific questions to stay present.
- Check in with annoying employees, especially when you have not heard from them recently.
- Keep track of materials and documents, and make sure they tie back to what was discussed previously.
- Introduce the short meeting format.
- Institute the peer meeting format.

Tactic #2: Change the Relationship Dynamic

"Obviously, our customers aren't trying hard enough!"

Managing Annoying People, 2017. By **Ilene Marcus**

Clear communication regarding your level of frustration and the impact it has on you, other employees, efficiency, and, in turn, the bottom line is essential. This is a major step toward getting the beast under control. If you don't communicate, there is a problem. How can it be tackled? Many managers believe they have communicated in annoying-subordinate situations. When truly analyzed, however, they realize they have not delivered a clear, direct sentence about how the manager experiences relationships with annoying employees.

This tactic focuses on what you can say to get your message across clearly and concisely to change the relationship dynamic. The goal is to inform the employee and the team that you have a relationship issue and to convey that you want to work together to transform this dynamic. You must talk specifically about the dynamic, not the work around it.

As you master the skill of recognizing these energy-draining, time-zapping beasts and their associated behaviors that impede your productivity and that of your team, you must be able to concretely discuss the dynamic. If you are not willing to have a conversation about the issue, then you are doomed to continue to repeat the behaviors.

Conveying the Purpose and Objective

The ideal is fierce conversation, a technique developed by Susan Scott, master teacher of positive change through powerful communication. The concept is to transform everyday conversations by employing effective ways to get your message across. You want your message to be heard, so it will begin to change the relationship dynamic.

Practically, you must state the purpose of the conversation for the talk to have any impact. This is a statement that is clean, neat, and simple. The goal is to be clear about the issue. You must be crystal clear that there is a relationship issue between the two of you.

This statement lays the foundation for the tactics you will use to address the situation. Conveying the purpose puts the employee on notice that you will be changing your behavior. Be clear about the behavior that annoys you. Be clear that it is a relationship issue, not a performance issue. The objective of this conversation is to change the dynamic of the relationship.

In her 2004 book, *Fierce Conversations: Achieving Success at Work and in Life One Conversation at a Time,* Susan Scott recommends these steps:

Susan Scott Steps	Managing Annoying People Example
Name the issue. In sixty seconds, make your opening statement about a behavior issue.	"You continuously interrupt not only me but everyone at meetings."
Describe a specific example.	"At yesterday's weekly team meeting, you would not let the HR person finish her report."
Describe your emotions about the issue.	"These behaviors frustrate me, so it's hard to listen to you, even though you are making important points."
Clarify what is at stake.	"This is affecting the productivity of the team."
Identify your contribution to this problem.	"It makes me react to you in a less thoughtful way."
Indicate your wish to resolve the issue.	"Starting with this conversation, I will address this issue directly."
Invite the subordinate to respond.	"Do you understand the behaviors I am addressing?"

The Setting

The physical place this conversation occurs is much less important than the emotional place. It should be calm, cool, collected. Keep an even tone in your words. Be open to listening, and be engaged in the conversation. You cannot just spit out your side of the issue and then revert to the behavior of trying to end the discussion because this person is so irritating. You may have this talk over the phone, especially if it's a remote employee. You cannot have this conversation via e-mail. Did I really even need to say that?

It's best to talk when both of you are in a good place. For example, you just got the green light for a project, had a meeting that increased your best client's order, solved a balance-sheet issue, or agreed on a new strategy for revenue development. The point is to talk when you are in a strong place and can both see the value of your work together.

Claire, Director of Professional Services

Claire, a true millennial and the director of professional services at a school for the developmentally disabled, had just finished a three-month project on comparative efficiency of her team of twenty-six therapists. She was overzealous and so excited about the information she now had, with which she could proactively manage underperformers. While we were discussing all the ways this information could impact operations, there was an opening, and I dove in.

"I would like to give you some feedback." As her manager, I didn't ask; I took the opportunity to give. "At times it's frustrating for me to manage you when you push your agenda items too hard, especially when your items are not central to the meeting. In our QA meeting last week, you would not move on from the scheduling issue. While I understand your concern, that issue could not be resolved with the QA team, and I was annoyed that the topic took away focus from the discussion. When a meeting gets off track, the entire team gets derailed, and the pressing issues do not get addressed. I was not stern enough with you in shutting down that discussion. I want to find a way for you to raise your issues in the proper setting without overpowering the rest of the team. What are your thoughts, Claire?"

Hone your Pitch

The absolutely best approach with an annoying energy zapper is to be direct. Short. Sweet. Direct. The tone should be honest, thoughtful, and unswerving. This should not be a long conversation, but it must be purposeful. Your emotions need to be kept at bay. This is a factual conversation. "I value you." "I appreciate your work." "I find it frustrating to manage you."

To stay even toned, remember that in life, events happen, and from an early age we quickly assign value to those events. For example, birthday party = good. Losing a job = bad. If we roll back our emotions and look at each event as just that—an event—and don't assign it a value, our opinions change. Everyone has been to a birthday party gone awry and, conversely, has said or known someone who said that losing a particular job was the best thing that ever happened. Our life experiences assign the good or bad connotation. Assigning a positive or negative charge starts with our tone and preconceptions. If you are even toned and factual, it is not bad or good; it just is.

Tom, Chief Executive Officer
Tom, the CEO, was frustrated with his team. They were all star performers, but the business wasn't meeting projected growth. Tom was annoyed because he believed the weekly

reports he received did not provide enough information. Jackie, an executive coach, was called to help Tom understand the disconnect between his communication and what his team was hearing.

After sitting in on several management meetings, the coach could see that Tom was in the habit of talking down to his team. Tom also started raising his voice as his annoyance escalated. Jackie coached Tom to address his behavior by engaging in a conversation about the reports instead of going through an intense interrogative process. When Tom addressed the team directly and calmly and started the conversation about the reports without charged emotion, it started a dialogue about the issues related to producing the reports and other indicators the team used and why. It started repairing the relationship and making the weekly meetings much more productive for the entire team. Within the next three months, the revenue projections were in reach.

Telling the Team

It takes a village. Cliché but true. As the leader you start the change and set the framework. You need all of your community rowing in the same direction to have a real impact. And your team closely watches your behavior toward them and the person (or people) you find aggravating. Through your reactions, you inform them about who is annoying you. Chances are most of them are feeling the same way. Now you need to show them how you can walk away from that behavior and turn the situation around.

You know your team and its dynamic, so it's up to you if you tell them individually or as a whole. Either way, the same rules apply.

Simple, direct, unemotional. Short and sweet. Explaining the impact that it has on you and the organization.

Ilene, Chief Operating Officer

As COO of a $20 million special-needs school, I managed a team of educators. The school principal hid behind regulations whenever she didn't want to do an assigned task. To combat this I would check the regulations and bring a copy with me to all meetings. Prior to employing the tactic of telling the team, my standard response went something like this: "Really? Because I don't see it in the regulations." I would bang my fist on the pile of papers next to me and then add for good measure, "As usual you are stating an extreme case. Who thinks this is an extreme case?"

A classic fight response, and the entire team would go on the defensive as I displayed my annoyance. Once I realized the impact of my conduct on the whole team, not just the intended recipient, I knew I needed a different tact. I started the next meeting by owning up to my behavior, opening with, "I have been annoyed at the slow pace of change and have lashed out at some of you. I am sorry. From today forward, this situation will be addressed by clarifying what is at stake if we do not change our behavior, and asking all of you, my senior team, to provide solutions to the issues raised. Would anyone like to add on to that or ask any questions?"

After that, the hallmarks of the meetings were cooperation, problem solving, and the team keeping me honest when I slipped back into banging on the regulations.

The COO learned you can't always fight.

Checklist: Change the Relationship Dynamic

- Keep your message short and direct.
- Use fierce conversation to be honest, direct, and purposeful.
- Choose a setting that is calming and neutral.
- Hone your pitch so you are not charged with emotion.
- Focus on transforming the team dynamic through meaningful actions.

Tactic #3: Set No Fear Boundaries

©Glasbergen
glasbergen.com

"How can you say we're not behaving like a team?
We're all wearing the same color shirts, aren't we?"

Managing Annoying People, 2017. By **Ilene Marcus**

We want to be fearless as leaders and executives. Being firm, standing our ground, staying composed, and getting what we need and want are distinct traits of leaders. Boundaries force distinction between entities and establish the relationship. Boundaries force efficiencies by defining the roles and responsibilities of each entity. Teams work more efficiently when everyone knows and plays the right part. As workplace warriors, we understand this. In practice, that's not always the case.

Subordinates, especially those you rely on due to specific niches or skill sets, can raise your temperature and impact your composure in ways that surprise you and catch you off guard. In one moment you let a behavior slip, and that makes all the difference. It's usually a small thing, such as the wording in a presentation or a change in the time of a meeting. You feel right away, in the pit of your stomach, that it is going to haunt you. And you know your gut is right, but it seems like a small thing, and you feel sheepish about going back on your word. Thinking about it you reason, once again, that it's just a small thing.

This is a boundary issue. Your subordinate crossed a line because you didn't set it, or it really was dotted to begin with, or it was just easier for you not to sort it out with that staff person. Boundaries create roles and responsibilities and dictate direction. Someone who annoys you to the point that you just give in or don't listen requires you to be fearless about setting boundaries. And often this happens when the whole team is present and sees it.

No Dots Allowed—Draw the Lines Clearly

Of course you are a good communicator. You would not be at the top of the food chain otherwise. And yet there are employees for whom the articulations of your exact concern, the nature of your intent, or your expectations seem to get lost or mistranslated.

An employee who falls into this dotted area (also known as a gray area) is special, usually because you have a connection to her. This is an employee you may have worked side by side with for a long time; maybe she now holds your previous position, or she has the same specialization as you. She belongs to a team of people you hired, or knew from previous jobs, and most likely you have been the champion of her department. The line is blurry because of this connection. It tends to make you more informal and trusting. And then boom, her behavior irritates you, and you realize meeting with her is sucking you dry. To stop being annoyed at her, you must be clear about your role and what you will not tolerate.

Kathy, Chief Financial Officer

Kathy is the CFO of a recruiting company. She is outgoing, warm, engaging, and funny. Staff interprets her style as informal. Kathy always has her head in the game. However, she is anything but informal. Cross a boundary with a joke or a too-familiar comment, and Kathy will let it slide. Cross a boundary with a work issue such as dealing with a difficult system or redesigning your department dashboard, and Kathy will put you right in your place. She sets boundaries clearly and provides constant feedback about where you stand and exactly what's expected.

Align the Context

As the leader in your company, it's your prime responsibility to provide the framework within which staff must perform. If you do not set the stage, the context of why, how, and what the company is driving toward, it can get messy. Providing a context guides actions and decisions.

A skilled manager becomes an annoying manager when he goes rogue with the best intentions and focuses on the wrong priorities. Setting the context for how each department's work will move the company toward the overall goals is paramount to making managers more efficient. Continuously aligning the mission, roles and responsibilities, and context for the work will keep both you and those you manage on track.

Noah, Business Owner
Noah is the owner of a large day care that is relatively unknown outside of the neighborhood. As part of its outreach and marketing efforts, he asked the Human Resources Department to look up reviews of the company on a recruiting website, to gain insight into the center's reputation. The HR director took the initiative to ask everyone who was interviewing as well as employees to write reviews. Suddenly the number of postings shot up, which looked suspicious.

If Noah had provided the context that parents are more savvy and use many indicators, such as how happy employees are at a school, to determine if it's a fit for their child, the HR director's actions would have been more purposeful and not resulted in a crafted-looking reputation campaign on a public website. If Noah had provided the context, the HR director's initiative would not have been a wasted effort.

Never Be Prey

In the Smoky Mountains in Tennessee, posted everywhere are signs that read BEAR AWARE. To sum it up it, when you encounter a bear, there are several things you should (or should not) do:

- Stand tall, shout very loudly, and stomp your feet.
- Make lots of noise.
- Do not crowd the bear.
- Give the bear a clear safe avenue of escape.
- *Do not run.* Back away slowly.
- Remember, bears will charge if they feel threatened.

All good advice, but it was the night manager at our hotel, Glenn, who said it best: "Stand firm. Bears can tell if you are easy prey." So can an annoying employee. If you are not fully present—if you are bored or making a to-do list in your head and just going through the motions of paying attention—you will be prey. These are the situations where you wind up asking yourself, "Why did I agree to that? Did I really say that? How did we get here?" You might also be saying, "I don't remember that conversation," because you were checked out. Either way, you become prey.

Jacob, Managing Director
Jacob has a tendency to tell a whole story and not to focus on the critical elements that require input. The CEO and his entire team find it frustrating and time wasting. As I was the CEO's coach, he confessed to me that he has learned to plan his "honey do" list during this time but chime in appropriately. The CEO is used to this pattern and believes that since all of his managers are around the table, the important items will be noticed.

Then it happened. After the last management meeting, the CEO was copied on a memo to all staff. Subject: "Join the CEO and senior team for the corporate challenge and a night of company bonding." The CEO said, "All I could think was, "How did I miss this?""

Checklist: No Fear Boundaries

- Establish clear boundaries between managers and subordinates.
- Set the expectations and intent.
- Align context to provide employees room to take initiative while working within the company framework.
- Pay attention, or you will be prey.

Tactic #4: Guard Your Time

©Glasbergen
glasbergen.com

"Of course I'm doing something about
the problem — I'm avoiding it!"

Managing Annoying People, 2017. By **Ilene Marcus**

In the attention economy, time is one of the most precious commodities. Employees who get under your skin and annoy you are highly correlated to lost time. These employees are devouring your most valuable resource. You must be the master of your schedule and guard your time like you are a mama bear and it is your baby cub. Once it's used, you cannot make more.

Given the magnitude of your commitments, you don't have any hours in the day to lose. Subordinates who are annoying tend to take even more of your time than others do. However, it's not only the chunk of hard time that they use, such as asking questions during your twenty free minutes or always going over their allotted meeting slot. It's the energy drain and then the recovery period you need as well. The scenario goes something like this: you don't want to see this specific person who is part of your team and you directly manage. But you know she is working on an important project. You have a meeting scheduled with her early next week. Even so, she has been hovering at your door enough for you to notice. There are also several pesky "checking in" e-mails that you have ignored or superficially answered. You reason with yourself that it will be a quick meeting, and you just have to push through it. This is a huge mistake. Just getting through it can often sabotage you for a lot more than a quick meeting; somehow it gets you off track for the next few hours or even the better part of your day.

Being the master of your time and calendar sounds simple. It gets messy when you are not attentive about owning your schedule. You are not in the habit of micromanaging your own time. You believe that your direct reports should have access to you to do their jobs. You know that your team works hard, and they all value their own time as well as yours as their manager. This is an active phase wherein being vigilant about setting the pace and tempo of encounters with annoying subordinates matters.

Time Check, Please

First things first. You must have a working time device. Your phone, a watch, a wearable—something you have with you at all times. Especially if you work in a school, restaurant, or field setting and do not sit in an office or have meetings in conference rooms. This holds true when you conduct meetings at the local Starbucks or remotely, when an old-fashioned wall clock or a clock on your tablet or computer screen may not be available. Either way, it's imperative to have a time device that you can see. Get used to looking at it. Be aware: if checking handhelds in meetings is not in your culture, that won't work unless you specifically state to meeting participants that you are using your handheld as a clock. You must be able to measure the time, or it will disappear.

This is particularly relevant for the subordinate who knows you are avoiding him. The same one who always catches you in the entrance or walks into your office just as your assistant has to run to another department; as your last appointment is walking out; or after hours, when no one else is around.

Mentally make note of the time the meeting starts, or, if you can, write it down. This is a reminder to watch the clock.

Richard, Chief Technology Officer
Richard ran the IT Department when I was running a large social-services agency with over 250 staff on-site and 3,000 more in the field. We were on the twenty-first floor, and he would always catch me in the elevator early in the morning, when I needed to gather my thoughts or think through an upcoming issue. Hellos and pleasantries weren't enough; Richard knew his facts and figures and took his elevator pitch seriously. His radar was flawless, and he always found me when he couldn't rest his millennial mind and needed to hammer a point. Always when I just needed some space. That was a big part of why I found him so irritating.

Nodding and not listening to him had backfired in the past. Direct and honest was the best approach: "Richard, I have literally thirty seconds to listen to your pitch, right? Right now is not the time to discuss this. You are welcome to ride along with me as long as you can keep it to thirty seconds; otherwise take the next elevator, and we can pick this conversation up at the management meeting this week." Tough but direct. Mama bear guards her time.

Set the Alarm

Figure out ahead of time how you will set the alarm. There are an infinite number of ways to do this: check your watch; actually set an alarm on your phone, tablet, or computer; have your administrative assistant or someone else remind you. You get the point. You must track the time. Sometimes there is an outside force that can be a reminder—a church bell, a shift-change clock, or a firehouse siren that goes off at the same interval throughout the day and can serve as a measurement.

Jennifer, Director of Nursing
While in charge of a $130 million nonprofit, I truly enjoyed talking to my director of nursing, Jennifer, who ran $80 million of the business. The best part was hearing her stories about what was going on in the field. She was extremely competent; crisis situations were few and far between, and we covered operations in our weekly meetings. These impromptu discussions were informative.

The downside: she was a time vortex. So I set up an alarm every half hour on my smartphone. It made it so easy to tap and start timing. The waterfall ringtone that sounded when time was up was a gentle reminder that my day would crash around me if I didn't limit my time with her.

Even when you like your team members, they can eat your precious time.

Own the Timetable

Right at the outset of a conversation or meeting, set the timetable. This includes the amount of time allotted, how you would like it organized, and how and when the meeting will end. Obviously this is neater when it's a scheduled meeting and not an encounter in the hallway, but the tactic works either way.

Start the conversation as follows: "We have forty-five minutes today to discuss topic XYZ. I have divided the agenda into three major parts—status, discussion on complications, and actions moving forward. Let's keep to this outline, use fifteen minutes for each section, and end promptly at the forty-five-minute mark, at X o'clock." In an informal setting, you can say the same.

Here's the kicker. Once you have set the timetable, ask, "Do you need a minute to organize your papers and thoughts to align with the agenda that's been set?" This lets the person or team know it is not business as usual and that he or they are expected to behave in the manner you have identified. Often the response will be lots of fumbling and then, "Oh, I thought we would do it this way," or, "I wanted to talk about A and B instead of XYZ." Stay the course, and let the other party or parties know they have already eaten into their allotted time with you.

If it's a random meeting, you can still say, "I am on a tight schedule," or, "I literally have five minutes, so get to the point quickly." Many people cannot do this. They start at A to tell you about B, so they can next bring up C—the issue they really need to talk about. This wastes your time, especially if you are familiar with the issue and know the track record of this person.

Ryan, Vice President of Human Resources
Ryan was responsible for hiring twenty new staff a month for a financial-services company. He was in the habit of pinging his boss Stanley every hour—"Need to meet you"; "Want to check

in"; "Important issues need your input." It was his annoying way of telling Stanley how busy and important he was; also, it was very irksome. At their regularly scheduled meetings, Ryan sucked up the first fifteen minutes recounting everything he'd done with way too much minutiae and showing Stanley how hooked into the office news he was (which the boss found even more annoying). Stanley set the timetable with Ryan and then asked him to start at the end. This threw Ryan for a loop; it forced him to focus on the end point, or the items he needed his boss to make decisions on. Meetings with Ryan transformed into thirty minutes and not full hours, and Stanley got the data and information he needed, not an inventory of how many phone calls and other actions Ryan had taken.

More than Time and Place

Actively thinking about the underlying forces that contribute to the success of a meeting is a good use of your time, and it is a skill. As managers, we often have this is as an intuitive skill. Breaking down the instinctual aspects and then doing purposeful planning around them can add dimension and lead to a better outcome.

Several factors contribute to defining the schedule to hold productive meetings. Elements to take into consideration go far beyond the time of day and place—your office or mine? When you're in the habit of guarding your time, many factors should inform your decision. Only you truly know the factors that matter to you or impact you, but here is a list to start with: the urgency or importance of the subject, the true amount of time needed to cover the material, its priority against other demands you are juggling, time of day that you best perform in this type of meeting, and the type of space conducive to the conversation.

Understanding your behaviors and when you can best tolerate or dominate the situation requires your honesty. This may sound familiar: "I know I shouldn't let my COO irritate me, but he does when he pulls out twenty dog-eared reports, and he knows I haven't read them." Decide if this is a meeting you dread, and if so, what will get you past it? Determine the factors that can contribute to you having an efficient meeting. For example, is it better to do it early in the day? And what type of meetings or tasks should be scheduled around it? Is this the type of meeting you need to hold off-site? Do you need to prepare prior to the meeting?

The considerations may change based on the particular employee, the time of year, or outside factors beyond your control. Either way, if you truly pay attention and think about what will make this the best meeting possible, even if it's a weekly one on one or standing management meeting, it will save you energy.

Judith, Director of External Relations

Judith was in charge of twenty-five community-based agencies for an umbrella nonprofit that provided front-line social services to over one hundred thousand clients a year. We met weekly, and she always presented facts and figures yet never included a clear-cut course of action. I consistently got annoyed because as we discussed options, she would produce yet another new piece of information from the seven-inch pile of folders and reports she always carried.

After several crashes and burns, I analyzed my instincts about meeting with her. I knew she enjoyed meeting in my office, and it was less preparation time for me, but I made the decision to move this meeting into the conference room. In this setting she could lay out all of that supporting documentation on the table, so we could peruse it and use it as we formulated an action plan. Laying those reports and charts across the table changed the entire meeting dynamic, from circling around issues to making decisions, action plans, and due dates.

Fill Up Your Schedule

If you are the type of manager who has regularly scheduled meetings with your staff, then this is important. Actually it's the only kind of manager to be. Managers must have consistent contact with direct reports. This becomes draining with staff members who suck your time. To combat this trap, it is essential to make sure you do not have open blocks of time before or after these meetings' scheduled slots, be they virtual or in person.

This is the "sandwich" method. It works particularly well if the subordinate is a top performer but has the habit of eating into your time. Never schedule this person's time as a standalone, without anything before or after it on your calendar. Make him or her middle of the sandwich. The formula is a meeting before and after, and the annoying person's meeting is in the middle.

Make this regular meeting part of your morning rounds. For example, every Wednesday I meet with key staff between 8:30 a.m. and 10:30 a.m. They should know their slots and understand that if they take more time than allotted, their colleagues are slighted. Never make the annoying employee the first or last meeting. Another tactic that works well is to schedule him or her right before a team meeting or when others are waiting for you, so you have a true escape route.

Eric, Deputy Commissioner of Facilities
In one of the largest NYC bureaucracies, Eric was as in charge of facilities, responsible for retrofitting 32 sites throughout the five boroughs under an extremely aggressive timetable for completion. His belief was that he should be given "extra" time to meet with me. Eric was competent, performed well,

and had run his division for nine years. He didn't need the extra management time. He just thrived on face time (which was annoying).

Cognizant of the fact that I needed to keep Eric motivated but also needed to guard my time, which I was balancing against heady policy discussions, union discussions, and day-to-day operations, I scheduled his weekly meeting right before our weekly management meeting. This was extremely effective. Eric felt that since he was the last one to get to me prior to the team meeting, he could shape my ideas, fitting his need to be seen and feel important. And we both had a hard stop for the management meeting.

Motivating and limiting time at the same time—that's a lesson.

Know Your Team's Comings and Goings

There are times when even the most dedicated employee draws the line and leaves his post. Figure out how to use this to your advantage. Akin to this are the times when those dedicated employees ask you to adapt to their schedules. Because you want to accommodate your team, you are often tempted to make time when you don't have it. Don't do it.

There are several scenarios that play out with your team's comings and goings. First, there are times that they will ask you for the squeeze in: just see them for a quick issue and then you don't have to worry about rearranging your whole schedule. This seems like a good approach for the annoying subordinate. Less time should yield less annoyance. This is never a good idea. It will squeeze your time and his. You shortchange the issue, and it will never be enough for the time sucker. It will cost you more time in the long run—the time you wasted on the squeeze in, the additional time you needed to set and address the issue, and the time you spent being annoyed that you squeezed him in. Often you also spend time listening to him complain about how you shortchanged the time he feels he needed.

There are times when pleading will be involved. The annoying subordinate may ask you to change your schedule so he can have more time to work on the analysis or be able to work at home before he leaves for that business trip. As a manager you probably know more about your team's personal relationships and habits than you care to. This does help you relate to them; however, it is not your responsibility to work around their schedules.

There is also the rule of "Just say no." There are several variations on this theme. Just saying no is the quickest, most straightforward, and most concise. No is a complete sentence all by itself. "No, I do not have time to meet with you this week." "No, I cannot accommodate your schedule this week." "No, I cannot change the time of our standing meeting."

By far, the most productive solution is to use their comings and goings as your advantage. For you, to get the benefit of a strict hard stop so you, can get back to your priorities.

Larisa, Budget Director

Larisa was fanatical about her favorite yoga class, which was held every Monday evening, so I knew there was no way she would stay late. As budget director for a very large city bureaucracy, Larisa worked an aggressive fifty-five to sixty-five hours a week. Monday nights were not negotiable for her. So, sometimes I may have chosen to schedule meetings at the end of the day on Monday, when I knew she would be making a beeline for the door. This kept the meetings on track and the annoying time sucking to a minimum.

Get Outside Help

As a CEO or C-suite executive, you know how to be commanding in your own right. However, there are times when you do need help with simple tasks that really aren't simple. You are meeting with an important customer after regular business hours—how do you get them a coffee? An emergency package needs to be shipped—how can you get it to the mail station quickly? Don't be shy about asking for help, and think outside of the box and your comfort zone. Especially if you work late or early, those who can help you may not be your usual suspects. In most offices the maintenance and security crews can be your best allies. Or the help can come from a team member you trust to get needed information or handle the situation. Your helper doesn't need details, just to understand that you have delegated an issue to him or her to handle. Although you may not use this outside helper often, once this person is authorized to take control, when you're in a crunch or a bad pattern, he or she can be a lifesaver. This works, as the person sucking your time and annoying you now sees himself or herself vis-à-vis another. The right help reinforces your message: "Not now." The other person can help in several ways. Foremost, if you've been reading and paying attention, you now that how you react is everything. With another person present, you will be more vigilant about your tone, actions, and level of annoyance. Likewise the annoying person usually acts differently when another is involved. They may temper their behavior or exaggerate it. If tempered, check yes—mission accomplished. If exaggerated, use the opportunity to address the behavior. As the manager, you take the lead and communicate: "I have asked so-and-so to join us in this discussion as I am irritated and it seems so are you from your behavior." The other person can provide support as well as a diversion for your actions.

In tandem with getting outside help, institute the handoff and end the conversation. Many people refer to this as "walking them to the door" or liken it to saying, "Don't let the door hit you on the way out." Getting up and walking to the nearest escape route with a firm "thanks" usually ends the time suck right there. If you have an outside helper, add, "And now so-and-so will take it from here."

Hope, Compliance Manager
Hope, a compliance manager for a regional health-care system, is very good at her job. She does have the tendency to talk very fast. She is a natural strategist and needs to go over all aspects of an issue. Good staff members are annoying when they ramble on and on and on. I prefer she field-test her theories prior to discussing them with me, as I found that otherwise she wastes my time. When she corners me, I walk her to the door and say, "Did you run this by Andrew, our HR head?" Andrew, per my understanding with him, then takes Hope's idea off my plate and points out its pitfalls to her straightaway. This saves the whole team time.

Checklist: Guard Your Time

- Use a working time device to measure the time suck.
- Set an alarm, and let it end the encounter.
- Own the timetable up front, and stick to it.
- Consider all the factors that contribute to a successful meeting.
- Utilize the sandwich method.
- Know your team's schedule, and use it to your advantage.
- Learn how to walk a time sucker to the door and hand him or her off to a trusted helper.

Tactic #5: Monitor Your Nonverbal Body Language

©Randy Glasbergen
glasbergen.com

"Good meeting. I totally agree
with everything you didn't say."

Managing Annoying People, 2017. By **Ilene Marcus**

Every morning we take time to check the mirror to ensure our clothes fit right and don't have stains. Some of us do it several times during the day (it's OK; everyone in the C-suite is just a tad narcissistic).

We don't usually spend time checking our facial expressions, mannerisms, or hand gestures. Yet our nonverbal body language clues us and others in to our emotions and where they might lead. Our emotions are literally visible without uttering a word.

On a random day, a Google search for "body language" returns 481 million results (in 0.54 seconds), yet most of us ignore body language until we are facing it head on, usually in a presentation that was videoed, a conference room with a wall of mirrors, a professional-development training with video feedback, or a homegrown video from a wedding party. We vow to address it, get a coach, take a class, and remember never to wear that jacket again...and then "ism" takes over. ISM stands for incredibly short memory. Even when we have information (in this case, tangible information in video form) it's easy to forget about it and act the same way again and again.

Check Yourself

Nonverbal behaviors are almost infinite yet are particular to each person. One person may smack her lips or blink excessively when she gets excited. Another can cock his head or slump his posture. As a first step, you must identify your nonverbal signals. What automatically kicks in for you when you're in an annoyed state? Signs of annoyance usually include slumped body posture, higher voice pitch, quicker talking pace, jumpy body movements, and shifting weight if standing. Figure out your signs and your triggers to master them.

Brenna, Chief Executive Officer
Brenna is the CEO of a large public-relations firm. Her chief revenue officer (CRO), Shari, was extremely driven, produced great results, and was an excessive talker. Brenna needed to listen to what her CRO had to say because she provided great

insights into the market, with data Brenna needed to use in her daily conversations. However, Brenna found the CRO's fast talking so irritating that she never sat down when they were in conversations. Brenna's nonverbal style when she was irritated was to sway to and fro. Once she identified this behavior, she made a conscious effort to sit down while talking to her CRO. Brenna also made a practice of being open [explained later in this chapter]. By changing her nonverbal annoyance, she actually changed her ability to listen and take in more of the information the CRO was spurting.

Do you see yourself? This CEO did not.

Meaningful Nonverbal Behavior

How you sit, where you stand, what you hold in your hand—a pen, a phone, or a paper—all impact how the person you are talking with perceives you. When your pulse quickens and your emotions kick in, you believe no one else notices. Nonetheless if you believe you are hiding your annoyance or disinterest, think again. Particularly because they are your employees, they notice. Your behavior communicates how invested you are and how much attention you are paying to their words and their concerns.

Laurie, Manager at a Medical Practice
Laurie managed a large home-visiting medical practice. The key to the business model was twenty minutes for each doctor to get in and out of each home. Many patients felt that the doctors rushed them and that all their concerns were not addressed. They were losing patients. Laurie, the practice manager, had to find a solution.

Dr. Robie always had great reviews; his patients loved him, and he was always able to keep to his twenty-minute schedule. He was able to see all his patients on time each day. Laurie asked him his secret, and he replied, "The first thing I do when I enter a patient's home is shake his or her hand, then I put my bag on the table, and I take my coat off and make a point of hanging it up. At the end of the visit, I make a point of putting my coat back on." Dr. Robie's nonverbal behavior of taking his coat on and off demonstrated to his patients that he was fully present for them.

This manager knows actions do speak louder than words.

Blending

Dr. Rick Brinkman and Dr. Rick Kirschner, in their book *Dealing with People You Can't Stand*, coined the term *blending*. Blending is how well you acclimate to the behavior of the people around you. For example, if they talk fast, you talk faster; if they sit, you sit; if they tap their feet, you tap your pen. The doctors believe that if you mimic a person's behavior just enough, it makes that person more comfortable and leads to his or her feeling of being better heard or understood.

While we don't want to mimic or blend with people's more irritating characteristics, we do want to mimic their behaviors to get better results, such as being heard and getting what we need out of an interaction.

Jeanne, Marketing Director
Fred, an account manager, likes to meet in the conference room. This truly irritates Jeanne, his boss and the marketing

director. Even if they are discussing a routine issue, Fred prefers to walk to the conference room, sit, and do it there. Jeanne gets irritated as it wastes her time, and she doesn't have access to her papers or notes. And aren't those rooms for real meetings?

After trial and error, Jeanne learned that when she met with Fred in the conference room, it was much more of a productive meeting. She got better results with shorter meetings. By blending with Fred's behavior and taking the time to walk with him and sit across from him, Jeanne actually got less annoyed with him and much more accomplished. Jeanne learned to leave her office to have a productive meeting.

Smile Like You Have a Secret

Most people (of course, you are not most people) think of having their arms crossed as the only nonverbal clue. Smiling is a great asset in the how-to-manage-an-annoying-person tool chest. When I smile like I have a secret, it changes my persona. Try it now. Smile like you have a secret. You can feel it in the pit of your stomach; you are lighter, more open. And, if you haven't noticed, it's hard to look down when you are smiling. Smiling forces you to raise your eyes to others' levels.

Carol Kinsey Goman, PhD, international keynote speaker on the impact of body language on leadership effectiveness, says, "Whenever I give a presentation on the impact of body language in the workplace, I always include a section on the power of a smile. That's because research shows that a smiling expression sends feedback from your face to your left frontal cortex, which in turn triggers the release of the neurotransmitters serotonin and dopamine into your brain. These 'happiness' chemicals begin to improve your mood."

Start the mental reaction with a physical activity. Smile.

Dan, Chief Operating Officer

Dan was a veteran of the C-suite. He had recently inherited the Communications Department, and managing the public-relations director was driving him insane. Courtney had a huge portfolio and was enthusiastic about her work. She also believed that there would never be bumps in the road and got extremely frustrated when things didn't work as she planned. Dan's style was to mentor and educate his direct reports. At first, he took great lengths to explain to Courtney how policies can be unevenly implemented. The major sticking point with Courtney was that there was missing data and she couldn't get past it. Dan explained to her several different ways that it was the Communication Department's job to fill in the blanks and build a cohesive story for the missing information. Courtney continued to harp on this point. Dan's frustration grew. The lengthy supervisory conversations became a weekly chore and a pain point for Dan. Dan employed the tactic of smiling like you have a secret, and right out of the gate, he felt the interaction was different. As Courtney started asking questions, he smiled the secret smile, the knowing smile. The smile uplifted Dan, and he felt relieved instead of irritated. He realized he didn't have to have all the answers or take his time to mentor her on internal office operations. This saved him time and energy, and had no differential impact on Courtney's behavior.

Even an experienced manager can learn to smile and not be annoyed.

Zip the Lip

Wisdom comes in many forms—for example, in sayings such as, "God gave you one mouth and two ears for a reason." Listening is not the same as not talking, but there is a ratio to be applied here: one mouth to two ears.

As managers we are used to doing the talking, so not-talking is a change. The power of not-talking is that it forces the other person in the interaction to think (if he or she even notices) and that it calms you internally. Not-talking, to address your anxiety, annoyance, or other feelings, helps you to measure your words, slow down, and think about what is really important in this interaction. Not-talking makes you more strategic, more important, and more purposeful.

How do you learn to measure your words? As C-suite execs, we are the alphas. Why would an alpha wait to speak? I have to ask myself: Does it need to be said? Does it need to be said by me? Does it need to be said by me right now? *Right now* is usually the defining factor. I have to trust my team enough, even when they annoy me, to let them finish their ideas, thoughts, and sentences.

Michael, Senior Business Development Manager
Michael was successful in business development. He was not scared to try anything and everything. As his manager, I knew this could get expensive. When I blew my budget, I got annoyed. Michael's ideas also annoyed me. When I am annoyed, I don't let the other person talk. I shut him down before he gets past go. I did this with Michael. One day I shut down one of his ideas…that was then implemented by another company a few months later and left our product in the dust. Who was to blame, Michael or I? Hard lesson to learn. I had to learn not to speak.

Not listening can be expensive.

Breathe

Stress is a human response that is intended for survival. It can also spur creativity, help you solve problems, and let you know when you are in trouble. It is undisputable that when you breathe, muscles relax, your framework shifts, and the sensors in your brain put the brakes on the flight response. Scientific research shows that in as little as three to five minutes, you can change your level of stress as it relates to anger, tension, and frustration. Bully for scientific research, but this person in the chair next to me is driving me crazy in *this* minute. It's not a flight-or-fight situation; it's a management meeting. As the boss and senior professional here, I need to get my stress into alignment immediately.

To accomplish this, take three deep breaths. *Seriously.* Starting from your stomach, breathe in, feeling your chest rise until you cannot fill up anymore, then hold it at the top. Exhale all the way, till it feels like your navel is pushing against your spine. Tell the truth: you felt it. Do the same thing again. One more time. Three deep belly breaths. Now, where were we?

Practice "I'm Open"

Our body language conveys our feelings and thoughts. Practice saying yes with your body language. Nonverbally communicate "I do hear you" rather than "I am in charge, and I can't wait till this meeting or conversation is over." Being open is different from listening. It puts your whole body into the game. Instead of sitting forward, ready to pounce, sit back and take it in, knowing that your chance to pounce will still be there to take if you need it.

Body language experts Allan and Barbara Pease's research reveals that when volunteers listened to a lecturer and folded their arms, not only did they learn and retain 38 percent less than the volunteers who maintained their uncrossed arms, but they also had more critical opinions of the lecturer. Crossed arms are a garden-variety nonverbal clue to your state of openness. Figure out how you and your body react to not being open. Communicate to your employees on both verbal and nonverbal levels that you are engaged, interested, and, most importantly, not annoyed.

To practice "I am open," sit in a chair in front of a mirror for ten minutes with your arms by your sides. Look into your own eyes. Stay still. Repeat. Repeat. Repeat.

Checklist: Monitor Your Nonverbal Body Language

- Check yourself with a body scan, and release your poses.
- Be meaningful with your nonverbal actions.
- Blend with others' nonannoying habits so that they can hear you better.
- Smile like you have a secret.
- Listen. Don't talk; don't plan. Listen.
- Breathe deeply and repeat.
- Practice "I'm open" and "I am here and unannoyed."

Tactic #6: Build Consistency

©Glasbergen
glasbergen.com

"Sometimes I like to walk past your desk without criticizing you.
Just to see that funny, confused look on your face."

Managing Annoying People, 2017. By **Ilene Marcus**

Consistency is a pattern of behavior that is sustained over a period of time. The ability to stick to your course of action is paramount to success in most endeavors. The arts of management and leadership are inextricability tied to your ability to innately size up a situation and apply the right tactic at the right time. With an annoying subordinate, whatever tactic you employ, it must be consistent to produce the intended impact.

The secret of most successful people is this little trick. Do it over and over again, whether you are in the mood or not. I once heard a famous songwriter say, "The trick is to be inspired every day. Mine strikes religiously at eleven a.m. daily." Consistency—not to be confused with routine—often gets short shrift. I don't want to be tied down; I became a CEO so it's someone else's job to be consistent, and it's my job to be inspirational. The true key to dealing with and overcoming any pesky problem is consistency. Find a tactic and apply it daily or even twice daily. Whatever it will take to overcome the situation.

Reliability

For consistency to work, the tactics you apply must be reliable. *Reliability* in a scientific framework refers to the ability to get the same results over and over again when applying the same tactic. For something to be considered reliable, it must be tested to get the intended result dependably. Consistency means that you do it. Reliability means you get the result you want each time you do it. For example, if you meet with your staff weekly, without fail, that's consistency. When each meeting produces the desired outcome, that's reliability. Holding the meeting doesn't guarantee a positive outcome; it guarantees an outcome. Reliability guarantees the outcome you desire if you apply the same process consistently.

The tactic you use must have reliability for it to be effective. Several factors influence reliability. Intent is a major indicator of reliability. Your driving intent, the full force that you use to implement your tactic, is directly proportional to how successful your tactic will be. Just going through the motions will not have an impact. Humans, especially smart, annoying ones, have good crap detectors. They can tell if you are muddling through the motions or if this is truly important to you. You must practice with intent.

Practice also impacts reliability. The more you do it, the more you can do it. If it's a conversation, the better you are at applying pressure at the right points, pausing for dramatic effect and sitting with the silence, the better the outcome. Making the tactic your own, your words, your mannerisms and practicing until it becomes part of your skill will ensure your results.

Proportional actions also impact reliability. You know the old saying: "Don't take a knife to a gun fight." Same here. All humans use intent to evaluate the seriousness of a given situation. We manage humans (although some are annoying beasts), and everyone eventually realizes where he or she fits in the food chain. Because employees will have intuitive knowledge of how important this is to you and how it fits into the business priorities, your response should be proportional and should mirror the situation.

Lucie, Director of Primary Research

In a large national television network, Lucie applied the tactic of filling up her schedule so that she never had more than thirty minutes alone with her director of programming, Franklin. This became the rule rather than the exception, and the relationship was on track. Lucie was now enjoying a good rapport with Franklin, and the work was going nicely. Lucie felt so comfortable that when she had some pressing meetings, she moved Franklin's meeting time. The first time this happened, Lucie felt the impact immediately. The meeting ran over, and Franklin agitated Lucie to the point that she had a headache and was late for her next two meetings. Lucie immediately changed the schedule back, and boom, the rules of the last six months were intact.

When it's reliable, don't go changing.

Responsiveness

At this stage in your career, you know when you are not getting straight answers to questions. When you ask your sales director, "How are those quarterly numbers looking?" and the response is, "Did you see our new ad in the business weekly?" your radar kicks right in. To make a finer point, you did get a response. It just didn't answer your question. It was nonresponsive. Responsiveness is the ability to respond directly to the issues presented. If what a person says doesn't relate back to the question asked, consider it nonresponsive. Responsiveness is a cornerstone of consistency. If you are not getting the intended results, consider that your tactic is nonresponsive. Particularly in human interactions, when you are engaged in conversation, it may be a delayed reaction that the answer did not respond to your question.

You must continuously be vigilant about responding to the behavior of annoying people and adhering to the course you have set to conquer it. You cannot let them off the hook because you know they will solve the issue, or because of their track record, or because chasing after them is too time consuming and annoying. You are the manager. Use the tools that work for you—for example, reports, e-mails, direct conversations, team infiltration, or an informant who gives you information to show the subordinate that he is not responsive to your management concerns, although the work is progressing nicely.

Reggie, Software Development Manager

Reggie was the hottest star at our company. The millennial had shot through the management ranks with the code he wrote that increased sales exponentially. Reggie was extremely driven and organized in his work and in the management of the entire coding team. His weak spot was talking to his manager, Brent, about problems as they arose. His young brain was wired to believe that he and his team could solve the problems without outside help or knowledge. And usually they did.

Since he hadn't been raised in organizational functioning, Reggie had trouble understanding that his manager needed to know the stumbling blocks to run interference, see patterns, and put it in perspective with other systems to see any potential impact. Explaining this, along with weekly meetings and new dashboard indicators, did not change Reggie's behavior. The manager recognized this as a responsiveness issue and adopted an approach that was tough to wiggle out of. The manager created a daily e-mail that required a response and all it said was, "Tell me three problems you faced today."

In the beginning Reggie answered the e-mail like a job applicant answers the question "What are your weaknesses?" Any good job applicant knows to answer this question with strengths disguised as weakness, such as: I am such a consummate team player that I usually don't get individual recognition; I love spreadsheets so much that I use them for everything, even when a simple chart will do. Reggie's answers sounded just like that: My team is so dedicated we found the bug in the code in only six hours. We rewrote a function for the client that he been complaining about for months.

Do you see the issue? Reggie's manager wanted to know that there was a bug in the code before the fix and that the customer was complaining. Reggie was not being responsive.

Brent tweaked the tactic to get Reggie to be responsive. Brent sent the e-mail every day at 5:00 p.m. and was stern with Reggie that he expected a response by 6:00 p.m. It took a few more days, but Reggie finally understood he had to be honest. With the short turnaround time, he really didn't have the time to spend on wording the e-mail. There are only so many ways you can say a negative as if it is a positive, even for a millennial.

Break the cycle of non-responsiveness with consistency.

Brutal Honesty

Not with the annoying person. Brutal honesty with yourself. If you cannot own up to the fact that this person is impacting your functioning, you will remain in the dark. Only you can decide when an issue has changed your behavior for the worse and impacted how you perform.

You cannot consistently manage anyone if you are not consistently vigilant about your state of mind so that your management style can be even-tempered and consistent.

To be brutally honest, you must be in touch with your feelings. You must know when you perform optimally. You must understand and pinpoint what impacts your optimal performance. You should know the type of people you work well with and those with whom you do not. There are an overwhelming number of work-style relationship assessments, including the Myers-Briggs Type Indicator® (MBTI®), the DiSC® profile, and the Kaleidoscope Profile®. Be warned: an assessment can predict real-world situations only to a point. The dynamics in day-to-day situations can be divergent with assessments and even prior relationships. You must determine when these relationships drain you or energize you. You must know the circumstances that lead to this behavior, so you can apply the tactics in a consistent framework.

Linda, Chief Executive Officer

Linda, CEO of a fashion company, always liked her CFO. They worked together for several years, and the company really grew over this time. This year Linda onboarded a new COO and felt energized after their meetings. The COO was proactive, brought data to the meetings, and focused on solutions instead of issues.

Eventually Linda noticed that on days she met with her CFO, she had more trouble focusing in her other meetings. At first she considered that there was a clue in the balance sheet. No. The time of day she met with the CFO? No. After trying several meeting formats and times, she had a strategic conversation with her CFO. Linda had to be brutally honest: the issue was her interactions with the CFO. In the early days, their styles had meshed; now, further along in her tenure as CEO, the CFO's style was not productive. Linda found hearing what was going on in the trenches draining. This relationship was draining. It took a new relationship for her to address with brutal honestly how she felt, what the triggers were, and what kind of impact they had on her performance.

When the CEO realizes one of her most trusted employees is now draining, it is time to take action.

Align Messaging

Consistency means your behavior must exemplify reliability and responsiveness. All of your interactions, phone calls, e-mails, elevator rides, and meetings with the annoying subordinate must be consistent. Your verbal and nonverbal behavior must match. Regardless of the time of day, you must bring full intent to the situation each and every time. Your leadership will be tested, and this is when it truly does matter. This is why you make the big bucks—to model the behavior consistently, be the leader, and show your employees how to work with you and, in turn, the entire company to be productive.

There are times when, in a crisis or white-cloud mode, we have a tendency to go with the flow and forgo being purposeful. If in crisis, we believe we will get back to our usual patterns once we get through. If it's a white cloud, we reason that our plan got us there, and the path will hold steady. Make a mental note about the annoying person, his behaviors, and your message and your plan.

Practice them religiously whether you are in a meeting, at a party, or on an airplane. Either mode—crisis or white cloud—can get you off track without a lot of effort. Your focus is to align your messaging across platforms and regardless of the ups and downs of the business cycle.

Reese, Director of Sales Operations

Reese, a division chief of a housewares manufacturer, is great company to Kyle, the CEO, at trade shows and out-of-town conferences. In the office it annoys Kyle that Reese sets up camp in her office and works from his makeshift command center. Reese does the same in her hotel room when on the road, and it's no bother at all. Kyle has been consistent in setting boundaries and letting Reese know he cannot pitch a tent in her office. Once Kyle acknowledged the pattern she noticed—that after a road trip Kyle was in her office more frequently—she had to set a new boundary for both on the road and in the office.

Don't Deviate

Winging it is not a plan. Figuring it out is not a plan. Depending on the situation is not a plan. A plan is a distinct set of actions that follow a course to achieve your stated goal. The goal is to have a blueprint of your actions when dealing with certain employees, so you can stay productive. If you don't have a plan, consistency is not possible. There are too many variables—the situation, other people, the time of day, pressing issues, and on and on. A plan can be as simple as "Just say no." A plan can also be as complicated as several actions, canned language, previously thought-of messaging, and a supporting cast.

Having a plan and executing it are two different things. You must stick to the plan. The bumper sticker would read PLAN YOUR WORK AND

WORK YOUR PLAN. Don't deviate. We all know the drill. We vow that today there will be no working late, and we will get to the gym or have dinner with a friend. Today I will hunker down and go through those reports or write that memo to the board. This week I will address that nagging situation with my annoying subordinates. What's different about today? Nothing, unless you have a realistic plan that you can truly implement.

The plan should have several elements:

1) Identify the trigger: when do you and your team start being counterproductive?
2) Choose a tactic: breathing, a peer-to-peer format, new boundaries, et cetera.
3) Apply the tactic consistently in your words, your actions, your e-mails, your calendar invites, and your meetings.
4) Monitor the tactic, and recalibrate or escalate based on outcomes and feedback.

John, Chief Strategy Officer
John, chief strategy officer at a tech company, likes to go over items at the end of the day with his boss the CEO. What they talk about is interesting. John is a good friend and has been a solid asset in quarter over quarter of smooth operations. The CEO likes to hear what John's team is up to and discuss ideas for their roadblocks.

However, the CEO started to see the pattern that if he had these conversations, as much as he enjoyed them, he wouldn't complete several items, and his entire next morning would be shot. What was annoying about it was that John often started these interesting discussions when the CEO felt pressed for time—that was the trigger. The CEO chose an active strategy, because this was high on his frustration scale. He used conversation to raise the topic and let John know this was an issue. And then the CEO said the magic words: "When I say I am pressed for time, please do not start a conversation, because I will not be able to finish it."

The CEO also used these words when he received a late-night e-mail with the subject "Just need a quick chat," an end-of-the-day "Just step into this team meeting and tell us what you think," and when John wandered into his office. The training was slow and steady. And consistency won the race. John and the CEO still have a great working relationship and find time to discuss what's needed—when the CEO is not pressed for time.

Checklist: Build Consistency

- Practice consistency, consistently.
- Force responsiveness to annoying behaviors.
- Use brutal honesty about what is triggering your actions.
- Align messaging across all interactions.
- Make a plan, and don't deviate.

Tactic #7: Know Busy Is Better

©Randy Glasbergen
glasbergen.com

GLASBERGEN

"There is no I in TEAM unless you disable auto-correct."

Managing Annoying People, 2017. By **Ilene Marcus**

Even millennials and pluralists know the tried-and-true adage, "If you want something done, give it to a busy person." Every manager worth his or her salt knows this to be true. The brave have tried to figure it out. This effect is multiplied in the management of those millennials and pluralists. They seem to have endless time to troll for information and endless patience to use a multitude of technology and devices. They look busy.

Looking busy is an art, and it has never been easier. In this instantaneous-information economy, there are more ways than ever to look busy. At work, it seems, a full 80 percent of daily routines involves looking at a screen of some kind or being in a meeting or in the field. As managers we all know the difference between the real thing and the imposter. It's that extra time on their hands without producing results that makes the competent imposters annoying.

The "busy is better" tactic accomplishes several goals. The primary one is getting the full value of what you pay for in employee time and effort. Secondary is the rule that increasing efficiency begets efficiency. Third is the impact on morale. If the kids are already playing nicely together, morale will be boosted. In a competitive environment, it raises the stakes across the players and teams. In a collegial environment, it actually relieves anxiety, as everyone does his or her fair share. In a dysfunctional environment, it shows your team that you truly know what's going on and are keeping the playing field level.

The true question is: what should busy look like? We all have dream projects and data we want at our fingertips. Getting your annoying subordinates to produce relevant, pertinent, and new work products can help you to see them in a whole new light and change the relationship dynamics while supporting corporate mission.

The Greater Good

As a leader it's important to set a tone throughout the organization that we are all connected. All work products should impact the greater good of the company. If one division or manager has implemented a better way, all should reap that benefit.

Busywork for the greater good is specifically designed for staff members or division heads who spend too much time worrying about how they compare to others, which irritates me incredibly. Behaviors can include sniffing around me, telling me all of their ideas all the time, showing up colleagues in meetings in order to be the center of attention, and not being a team player. I challenge them to use these annoying traits for the pursuit of good, not evil, to benefit the whole company.

Take your generic annoying employee who combs through reports all day to document the value of his specific division. He wants to show you that his division is really leading the sales team and painstakingly takes efforts to adjust the data for all types of variation (convincingly, I may add), including regional factors, work schedules, and market cap. The same annoying employee can use these powers for good by combing through the data and figuring out how all regions can succeed by analyzing the patterns in high-performing regions and pinpointing the actions that lead to those patterns. Now, that's the type of information I want to read, discuss, share, and, most importantly, use in day-to-day management.

Ally, Chief Analyst

Ally had her team crunch data daily and was a huge fan of sending Helen, the COO, end-of-day e-mails with stats. Helen found them useful—at first. Eventually she stopped reading the e-mails because they were not comparable with other divisions'. It was even more annoying when Ally continuously asked Helen why she was not reading her reports.

Helen had a conversation with Ally and suggested she create a template for other divisions and then train and implement the template across several departments. This would reveal stars as well as pain points. Ally did just that. This work showcased a hidden skill set of hers to her colleagues, and it provided useful information. Helen was most surprised that she now looked forward to the reports instead of wasting time looking at them and being annoyed with Ally.

Who doesn't love a template?

The Workout Files

All companies have them—useless files that you are mandated to keep. No one even knows if it's internal or external policy, but you must keep these files. We store them in locked file rooms. In old, torn folders in an empty cubicle. In scanned directories on our computers that take up space on the server. These are files your team inherited from the team before them. Everyone agrees they need to be retained, although they rarely have a clear status and owner.

Go give those files a workout. There are so many things you can do with them. Update the chronology; figure out the status; scan and create a directory. Remove them from the directory and store offline. The idea is that when these actions are delegated, you can actually tell what was accomplished. Where the files reboxed? Did the missing files appear? Was the status reviewed? Did we move them off-site for storage? Are they available electronically? Was server space freed up? This project has actions and outcomes. It's directly assignable and can keep a team busy for quite a while.

Rose, Managing Director

Rose was frustrated with the look of Dylan's office suite. His team was competent, but there were boxes and boxes of old project files. Many had sophisticated designs and budgets that served as the basis for a suite of current projects. All the items that were used regularly had been scanned in and uploaded as templates, but still the old, worn manila folders in tattered boxes lined each cubicle.

Rose asked Dylan to clean up because this mess demonstrated to her that working around obstacles was acceptable. Dylan started slowly, but as Rose become more responsive to him, he was glad he had taken on the project. It never occurred to either of them that their relationship was stale because she was annoyed by those boxes.

The Wild Goose Chase

A wild goose chase is a series of exercises designed to keep staff on their toes and to keep their work fresh. A mechanism to get your point across with a touch of absurdity that will unannoy you. A term coined by Shakespeare to embody a hopeless quest with lessons along the way.

Choose your favorite name—the wild goose chase, securing the wicked witch's broom, the *Star Trek* Kobayashi Maru test. It's all about the journey to have your staff prove their worth and prowess with a task that cannot be solved. The goal is to provide exponential learning during the process and hopefully discover why some employees are perceived as annoying. Keep annoying people busy and eager to prove themselves when it can't be done. That will keep them away from you for as long as need be.

The key ingredient is choosing the right project. This requires a delicate balance of importance, relevance, and specific knowledge that is not related to mission-critical outcomes at this juncture. Your ability to pinpoint what motivates an annoying employee and how to exploit this is the art of the chase.

David, Facilities Manager
It was the end of a long office renovation of over sixty thousand square feet—the size of a football field—with three hundred cubicles, fifteen conference rooms, and several common areas and closets. Many moving parts had been organized,

and David, the facilities manager, was used to having lots of face time with the CEO during the project. Now the CEO was finding the time David needed annoying.

Then the CEO saw the goose chase. The carpet tiles had been laid, but the excess was nowhere to be found. The whole point of using carpet tiles had been to easily fix sections that were soiled. They would eventually need extra tiles they currently didn't have. The CEO gave David the job of finding the perfect dye-lot match for the tiles that had been laid. The CEO knew that no other dye lot would ever match the one they had. He also knew that even if they had tiles in storage, they would never match those in use due to fading and usual wear and tear. What if the CEO just wanted to keep David busy and out of his office? David had to find that out the hard way after a long goose chase that put a lot of distance between him and the CEO.

The Easter Egg

An evolved twist on the Wild Goose Chase is the Easter egg. Described as an intentional inside joke, hidden message, or unexpected feature, the Easter egg originated as a surprise feature in a piece of gaming software included for those in the know. The phenomenon has now mushroomed and is in use proactively by companies such as Disney, Pixar, Google and Zappos.

Coveted by millennials who thrive on finding a back door, a secret and random clues, it's a safe bet Easter eggs will continue to be popular. In earlier iterations, this may have been a treasure map, the Holy Grail pilgrimage, or the search for the pot of gold. Actually, the Easter egg embodies all of those concepts and is a great management tool. Easter eggs can be an extremely effective team alignment strategy. In action, they bind together past and future projects and promote team bonding.

Marketing Team

At the ripe age of 30, a hallmark NYC nonprofit needed an updated logo. The current one in use didn't translate well online and was hard to read for print branding opportunities. The Board of Directors was at odds about this change, concerned that with a sleeker, cleaner look, the agency would move away from its roots. That's when the CEO directed the millennial marketing team to undertake an Easter egg hunt. The team visited every office, spoke to old board members and, old time staff, looked through ratty old paper files and found archival pictures that were synonymous with the existing brand. They plugged an old concept into a new logo and voila – an icon was born. The team built on the organization's past, for those in the know; they realized where the hidden picture was and connected it with the promise of the future. A perfect formula.

Checklist: Know Busy Is Better

- Choose good work product that support the entire organization for the Greater Good.
- Organize and use the old files that came from those before you.
- Keep annoying people busy and proving themselves with a wild goose chase.
- Increase team bonding using Easter Eggs.

CHAPTER 4

KEEPING THE ANNOYING PEOPLE AT BAY

"I am SO doing something — I'm making my coworkers look more productive!"

Managing Annoying People, 2017. By **Ilene Marcus**

Staying the course is a modern-day miracle. It's really easy to get distracted by priorities, customers, crises, and growth issues. The management of annoying people must be a persistent effort, given that they are persistently annoying people. When you act differently because someone annoys you and it is felt in your daily routine, it will eventually compromise the bottom line.

Once you have tamed the beast and gotten out of the trap, your strategy should turn to how to keep the beast on a short leash. Now that you have employed the tactics, you have figured out how to shape the perfect solution for each situation. To keep this relationship balanced and continue to reap results, you need a maintenance plan.

The idea of a maintenance plan is to keep the overall new structure and shape of the relationship with minimal pruning. Your goal is to sustain the results you have achieved with minimal effort. The maintenance plan includes the tactics you have used to date with additional tools to measure if the plan is still working.

Keep the Beast on a Leash

We all know and have experienced the saying "Fail to plan and plan to fail." Particularly after a good result with a new strategy, the plan becomes rote and then sloppy. We tend to believe it's just a blip, and it will turn back around. Your focus is to find the balance between when it is still working and when it starts to veer off track. That's the point when you go back for the refresher talk. If the refresher talk does not do the trick, then you will need to recraft the plan.

One thing about annoying people: they are very good at annoying you. So very often if you solve one issue, another issue will rear its ugly head. I call that whack-a-mole management, named after the carnival game where you keep putting those moles back in the holes with a bludgeon. It alleviates the immediate issue but doesn't change the playing field. As the manager you have gotten that person to retreat temporarily. The goal is to keep him or her from popping out of that hole.

Anna, Quality Assurance Manager

Anna was always late for her weekly one-on-one meeting, even though it was always held in the peer meeting, so she was not solo in these meetings. She always just had to finish one more critical thing. Of course as soon as her boss, Bruce, started talking to her peer, she would show up, and the three of them would play catch-up. Bruce found this extremely irritating. Wasted time.

Bruce discussed this with her and then moved the meeting to a forty-minute format from the scheduled hour time. Anna was upset she was getting so little face time for her important issues, and it was not even one on one, since his original tactic for her instituted the peer-meeting format. Bruce let her know if she had important issues, then it was important to be on time. The mole has stayed in the hole for quite some time now. And the meeting is still held in peer format and the shorter forty-minute format.

The CEO keeps that mole on time.

Role-Playing

Make-believe is annoying. Ergo, role-playing is annoying. I believed that for a long time. I am savvy; I thought I could handle what arose. Not true. Role-playing makes sure you see the unexpected. It's one of those phenomena of the universe that works and it's not clear how or why. Ideas or thoughts that may be out of your sight or mind, or are only subconsciously lurking, are brought to the surface during role-play. It's eerily real.

Role-playing is one of the most valuable planning tools. It's a little like improvisation comedy—you never know where it will take you, and very often it's far from where you began. We all get into groupthink when we feel good about a presentation or a project. We know how diligent we have been about the presentation. We've had our team analyze every aspect, fact-check all statistics, verify data. We review over and over in our heads how it will play out and what accolades are to come. We don't always take the time to stand in someone else's shoes and see what that person may see. Actual role-playing with another person can open up a whole new line of thinking.

Mckensie, Chief Executive Officer
Mckensie a CEO, was ready to talk to Bill, the COO. They had been colleagues for years, but their relationship had been strained for months, since she had taken over as CEO. She had followed the tactics and gotten their relationship back on track. But for the past month, signs of the old strain were showing. She was losing valuable time on market decisions because she felt Bill pushed back on whatever she said. She confided in her coach that Bill's insights were not wrong, but she was annoyed by this interaction, and it sucked her energy. It seemed to her he was challenging her position again.

Mckensie knew she had to have a new conversation with Bill—a refresher of the original talk. The coach suggested Mckensie role-play the conversation. Mckensie began, "Bill, it feels as though I am getting pushback from you the last few weeks, especially when we discuss compensation. It's frustrating to me, because the work is not progressing. I would like to discuss what's at stake and how we can get on track."

Role-playing Bill, the coach responded, "Absolutely. You know how dedicated I am to this company. It's just that my daughter has been diagnosed with anorexia, and the last few weeks have been devastating for us." Mckensie had not expected to be having this conversation and was unprepared. She was sure the issues had to do with the relationship between her and Bill. It had never occurred to her that this could be something personal affecting his engagement on the job.

Mckensie had known Bill for decades, but she didn't know everything.

Daily Inventory

Checking inventory is as common as breathing. We check the battery-charge level on our phones, the balances in our bank accounts, the number of e-mails in our inboxes and the stats on our wearables. As managers we are used to checking in on priorities and tracking progress. Most of us have systems that work for our industries or for us personally and keep us focused. Add your annoyance level to the inventory.

Annoyance level is the point prior to boiling. The point where you must make a decision, because your thought patterns, behavior, and actions are changing. It may mean you disagree with everything the annoying person says in a meeting, or you begin canceling meetings with him, or you find fault in items that are not egregious. The inventory forces thinking about the approach to your work and those nagging, messy issues that have been keeping you from peak performance. That annoying person who chips away at your calm, your priorities, your focus.

I use the following list to scan for actions I must take or those I do not want to take:

- Priorities: what must get done today?
- Hot issues: what is still pending or about to explode?

- Wants: what is my agenda for moving the company or project forward?
- Annoyance level: who is on my mind and wasting my time with no real results?

Checklist: Keeping the Annoying People at Bay

- Employ a maintenance plan to keep the beast under control.
- Use role-playing to figure out the bumps in the road.
- Take a daily inventory, and be honest about your annoyance scale.

CHAPTER 5

DEALING WITH ANNOYING CUSTOMERS AND VENDORS

©Randy Glasbergen
glasbergen.com

The Customer
Is Always Right
on the verge of making
me lose my mind!

GLASBERGEN

Managing Annoying People, 2017. By **Ilene Marcus**

You need them. Truly you do. Customers who purchase products and services from you. Vendors who provide you with the resources you need to generate income. Funders who support your work. Antithetical to the entire premise of managing people who work for you, the economic contract is reversed with customers and vendors. The entire relationship is based on the fact that you need the economic contract with them.

Without customers who pay you for your products or service—and, even further, are happy to pay for your products and services—you don't have a business. Vendors who are reliable and consistent, who don't gouge you, and who value the partnership are critical for your success. For each vendor you are the customer. The circle of commerce turns.

When you come across annoying people who are your customers and vendors, you will need tools to govern the relationships to address these annoying valued partners. When dealing with annoying customers and vendors, it becomes even more imperative that your team and those who work for you are not annoying you, wasting your time, and causing unproductive behavior. It's almost impossible to fight off an attack from all fronts. As the manager you clearly need to get your team in line, so you have the bandwidth to deal with the not-as-easy-to-clamp-down-on annoying customers and vendors.

You Are Not the Alpha

Even if you are the alpha (the dominant one), there is a power differential when someone is purchasing from you. Remember the basic rules of customer service, coined by Stew Leonard:

- Rule 1: the customer is always right.
- Rule 2: if the customer is ever wrong, reread rule #1.

Under these rules customers have a unique importance in our ecosystems. What happens when a customer or vendor is persistently annoying? Usually this has to do with style, communication, and the fact that you need this relationship. This makes it difficult to navigate, because you are not in the driver's seat. There are circumstances when your products and services are in high demand, and as a company, or in a particular region, you have not fully scaled to meet this need, so you cannot accommodate all orders and have a back-order list. But even in those times, it's highly unlikely that any company would turn away any customers.

Start by defining the relationship and understanding that there will be more give than take. Prioritize your needs, the cost of goods, customer potential, and the payment terms, and balance those with how much you and your team can manage in terms of the relationship needs.

Leslie, Founder

Leslie is the founder of an eyewear company, and Donna was one of her major customers. Donna had been an early adopter of Leslie's brand and came through with larger and larger orders. Donna had no time clock. She would call with a question and keep Leslie on the phone for nearly an hour talking about industry trends and needs. Whenever Leslie suggested a lunch or early-morning coffee, Donna balked and insisted it was just a short call. Over the course of six months, they logged fifteen hours, or two full days of work, with these "short" phone calls—very irksome. However, Donna was one of Leslie's biggest customers. Based on rule one and rule two, Leslie had to comply. She just had to make sure someone in her management ranks was picking up the slack.

The company founder remembered that for a good customer, time does stand still.

Stay Mission Focused

In a nonprofit, a union, an association, or a school setting, there are times when funders and grant makers may ask you for programs and services that may not be relevant to your core mission or may be too complicated and specialized to provide. This is a tough situation. Honesty is always the best policy.

Marianne, Director of Contracts
Marianne had to decide to twist into a pretzel or not. A community foundation had been a consistent funder of the human-services agency for several years. The foundation's new focus was on children of incarcerated mothers. The agency had several years of work with the mothers but not with the children. Marianne's initial response was to turn the grant down. She felt in a bind and decided to be honest with the funder. Marianne told them, "It's not what we were created to do, but at the same time it is a natural extension of our work, and the start-up would add considerably to the costs of operating a new program."

The funder did not give all the money but instead provided a seed grant to see if it fit with the model and to gain same expertise in that area before a final decision was made. If Marianne had outright said no, it's not clear what the impact would have been on the other grants this funder received.

Communication and Contact

I like plans. They provide frameworks with decisions already analyzed. Good plans provide maximum output with minimal effort. The key is the execution of the plan. You must stay in communication and contact with customers, funders, and vendors. Timing is also crucial. You want to be in contact with the customer when there are no issues, when you are not irritated, and when you have time to listen. The thing about annoying customers is they know when you are not paying attention. It's like radar; they home in on it. You also want to incorporate the "just because" call, so it doesn't look like you are on a calendared plan. Changing up the contact method breaks the monotony too. Switch between e-mailing, making phone calls, dropping in to a meeting when they are on your site, and making sure you run into them at industry events.

Rita, Chief of New Product Development
Rita had worked in this cosmetics company for years. She had a gift for keeping in touch with customers and vendors. It came naturally to her. As chief of new product development, she had not seen a client in over two years, yet not a one complained. Rita kept a ready-to-go e-mail list; at frequent but not perfectly spaced intervals, she sent updates on products and included personal notes. At our annual sales conference, it was clear that everyone felt connected to her as she sailed through the crowd, shaking hands and sharing lots of warm embraces.

Hype Your Team

Everyone wants to talk to the boss. As you grow your business and your customer base, not only do you have less time, but you have competing priorities to manage. It's always those who irritate you the most who insist on you personally handling their accounts. Unless you are a die-hard salesperson and this is your wheelhouse, as the boss, you will need a strategy to extract yourself from these customers. This is dependent on them trusting and feeling kindred with your team. Your goal is to put distance between you and the annoying customer while he or she still feels the glow of your relationship.

It seems to work best if you hype your team. Basically, sell your team to your customers. Let them know why you hired and trust these people. Explain the value a closer relationship with the team or person working with them day in and out would add to their businesses. Explain the worth it can bring to their transactions with your company. Communicate that you will have an internal plan to stay abreast of and informed about their accounts. Reassurances that of course they will always have access to you will go a long way when combined with the team hype.

The key factor in hyping your team is the handoff. Knowing your customers well and honoring your relationship and interactions with them must be considered. Only you and your team can determine the best handoff route to take. Just make sure there is a plan that fits with the customers' needs, track records, and styles.

Brad, Chief Executive Officer

Tony wanted to deal only with Brad, the CEO. Tony was an original customer, and it was Brad who had signed their first deal personally. They were cordial and liked each other. However, Brad had spent a full year building the capacity of his sales team and really needed to focus on product development. He knew his customer and set up a face-to-face breakfast at the Princeton Club, Tony's usual place. Brad let him know the direction in which the company was moving and that Trevor would be his new day-to-day contact. He hyped Trevor and let Tony know how much they had in common and how well they would get along.

Brad had also taken a risk and asked Trevor to arrange his schedule so he would be at the Princeton Club that morning. Timing was on their side, and on the way out they all connected. After small talk and introductions, Trevor went on his way; Tony turned to Brad and said, "Well, he likes the same club as me. That's a good start."

Recognize the Signs

Each customer has unique quirks. Sometimes you will need to proactively look for signs that although their relationship is on track, there may be something brewing. Know your key customers' and vendors' likes, dislikes, and quirks, and make sure your sales and operations team has a system for quantifying neediness.

Customer, Nervous Nellie
Robert knew that his best customer did not like change and was a Nervous Nellie when it was time to renegotiate pricing. The sales contract outlined a very clear pricing policy at twelve-month intervals. Robert knew he had to start the conversation about changes almost a full three months ahead of time.

When Robert was promoted and Joe took over the account, Robert laid out his action plan. Joe said he understood and would handle it. Joe and Nervous Nellie got along well, and Joe paid special attention to ensure that their collegial exchanges were enough to manage the situation. When the new pricing was sent over to Nervous Nellie, Joe took special caution to reach out and even had Robert call to cement the deal.

Checklist: Dealing with Annoying Customers and Vendors

- Awareness of the power differential should guide your actions.
- Stay mission focused, and remember that honesty is the best policy.
- Keep regular communication and contact—these are necessary and not evil.
- Hype your team to put distance between you and annoying customers.
- Recognize the signs of what each customer, funder, or vendor needs, and do your best to accommodate them.

CHAPTER 6

PERSPECTIVE

"Now that we've embraced our diversity, celebrated our pioneering spirit, made a fresh commitment to excellence and given something back to the community, does anyone remember what we do to make money?"

Managing Annoying People, 2017. By **Ilene Marcus**

We are born with aptitude. That's what got you here. Your acumen in reaching goals, ability to work with people, and to focus in on what's important. Some skills need coaching and nurturing. Professional athletes train, do skill drills, and practice, practice, practice. Even if you have been in the game a long time, it behooves you to continually hone your skill set. With millennials, pluralists, and who knows what's next, new ideas, capabilities, and talents are always needed to manage an evolving workforce.

The journey begins with learning a skill. The next step is to practice and finally to master it. Mastery comes with practice. Annoying subordinates can zap your energy at any time. Even in the mastery phase, annoying employees will give you a run for your money. In mastery, your ability to spot these annoyers, the time it takes you to get the situation under control, and your even-tempered ability to not let it get you off track will be the hallmarks of your leadership style.

Be the Model

Model the behaviors you value and that you know produce positive reactions and relationships in your workplace. Business priorities and cultures can shift. As a manager, the best tool you have is to be the best manager you can be and to model that behavior with each interaction. It's never the wrong time to be the best you can be.

Inspire

When direct reports take initiative while exceeding their current deliverables and produce extra work that predicts business-strategy questions, that's not serendipity. That's the result of management. Inspired management. That's always the goal: to create an environment wherein your employees can thrive because they see you supporting their work and dealing with any barriers (real or imagined) that get in the way.

Ride the Ride

The bumps in the road are not always fun, but they do provide comparisons for when there is smooth sailing. No one is ever perfect (although we keep trying). Each time we pick ourselves up and start again, we are better for it. As leaders we must smooth out the ride for our employees. It's our job to minimize drama and volatility in the workplace. When we join in the dysfunction, the ride gets wild.

Maintain Perspective

Metaphorically, it would be a shame if where you stood at the beginning of this book and where you stand now are in the same place. If they are, please call me directly.

Seriously, time heals all, and even as we learn to keep our composure and identify who and what annoy us, new challenges will arise. And why not? It would be boring otherwise. Progress is the act of moving forward. Stay the course.

Checklist: Perspective

- Model the leadership traits you value.
- Inspire your employees.
- Ride the ride, and make the road smooth and even.
- Maintain perspective, and make progress.

ABOUT THE AUTHOR

Ilene Marcus is a dynamic, results-driven leader with expertise in complex workplaces. From government to tech pioneer DoubleClick to large nonprofits as well as healthcare organizations, and product-driven small businesses, Marcus has been on the front lines and seen it all. Serving under New York City Mayor Rudolph Giuliani, Marcus spearheaded the city's historic welfare reform, impacting millions of dollars and people. With master's degrees from Columbia University in social work and public administration, Marcus has a unique skill set. In addition, she served as an adjunct faculty member at Columbia for ten years, teaching financial management to hundreds of graduate students.

Marcus now heads Aligned Workplace working with executive teams to tackle challenges, created by discontinuity in policy and economic shifts, and to focus on growth. Her signature products mentor leaders and managers to build powerful, engaged teams where success, inspiration, relevance, and kindness define the culture.

For more information, please visit www.AlignedWorkplace.com.

Made in the USA
Lexington, KY
29 May 2017